D0432603

LITTLE BOOK OF
WESTERNS

LITTLE BOOK OF

WESTERNS

First published in the UK in 2014

© Demand Media Limited 2014

www.demand-media.co.uk

Printed and bound in Europe

ISBN 978-1-910270-71-4

Contents

Introduction

In 1893, historian Frederick Jackson Turner argued that American democracy was formed by the American frontier, which liberated Americans from European mindsets and encouraged new ways of living. North America had a series of frontiers which fell as settlers gradually moved west, and the Wild West was its last frontier. Officially declared closed in 1890, the Wild West vanished with the appearance of the railways, the establishment of settled communities and the vanquishing of the Native Americans.

Although the Wild West existed for only a brief moment in America's history, it has fascinated filmmakers and audiences alike since the earliest days of cinema. Westerns, however, do not simply tell the history of a bygone era. Instead, Westerns explore the traits that Turner argues were cultivated by the fall of the Western frontier: courage, determination, camaraderie and honour. Of course darker elements also prevail, and many of the films in this Little Book are dominated by the desire for revenge and racial paranoia. These traits, both good and bad, are not of course unique to Westerns and indeed feature in much earlier works of art, such as Shakespeare's play *Othello*. What *is* unique to the Western is the depiction of the tight geographical and historical boundary of the Wild West: by returning time and time again to a single point in American history, filmmakers are able to produce endless permutations on the capacity of human beings to endure hardship and demonstrate valour.

The Wild West, then, is an epic stage for the tragedies of humankind:

films such as *Shane* (1953) that deal with hero worship or films such as *High Noon* (1952) that explore abandonment carry messages that resonate with audiences worldwide. However, in spite of the universal nature of the themes explored in Westerns, this genre has a unique aesthetic: when the Japanese film *Seven Samurai* (1954) was given a Wild West makeover as *The Magnificent Seven* (1960), the splendour of the American landscape, guns and clothing added a special flavour to the story. Gunfights, Apache war parties, cavalry charges: these are images not easily forgotten, and without doubt the Western is a stylish genre perhaps best summed up by the image of Clint Eastwood (above) in the Sergio Leone's "Dollars Trilogy".

People often ask "What is the best Western?" but this question is impossible to answer, as there are Westerns to suit every possible taste. Musicals such as *Calamity Jane* (1953) appeal to some people, while others prefer thrillers such as *The Missing* (2003). This *Little Book of Westerns* attempts to capture the wealth of stories and true histories that comprise the Western genre, and does so by gathering together accounts of fifty diverse Western films and TV series from the 1930s to the present day.

Alias Smith and Jones (TV series, 1971-1973)

Executive producer: Roy Huggins

The TV series *Alias Smith and Jones* was created in response to the popularity of the 1969 film, *Butch Cassidy and the Sundance Kid,* and makes numerous references to this cult film. For example, the central characters are named after the false identities invented by the Sundance Kid prior to a Bolivian bank raid, and actor Ben Murphy, who played "Kid" Curry in the TV show, resembles actor Paul Newman, who played Butch Cassidy in the film. *Alias Smith and Jones* attempts to recreate the laidback humour of *Butch Cassidy and the Sundance Kid* and each episode features attractive people in whimsical situations. Although highly successful, the TV series lost some of its feel good factor after the tragic death of lead actor Pete Duel.

Storyline

Alias Smith and Jones recounts the exploits of two repentant fugitives from the law, Hannibal Heyes (first Pete Duel, then Roger Davis) and Jedediah "Kid" Curry (Ben Murphy). Heyes is the mastermind behind the Devil's Hole Gang, but having fallen out with fellow gang members and finding a life of crime increasingly hard, he and his cousin Curry decide to go straight. Because they have never committed murder, the likeable outlaws are offered a pardon from the territorial governor on condition that they stay out of trouble and keep the deal secret for an unspecified period of time. Until then they are wanted men, so in order to evade detection Heyes assumes the alias 'Joshua Smith' and

Curry calls himself 'Thaddeus Jones'.

A life without crime proves harder to lead than Heyes and Curry anticipated, and they find themselves in a series of scrapes with bounty hunters, lawmen and other outlaws, including the Devil's Hole Gang. Fortunately they are able to rely on Heyes' brains and Curry's brawn to keep them out of trouble.

Bullet points

- The names "Smith" and "Jones" are borrowed from the 1969 film *Butch Cassidy and the Sundance Kid*. Prior to one of their final hold-ups at a bank, Sundance turns to Butch and says: "I'm Smith and you're Jones."

- The title was spoofed by the comedians Mel Smith and Griff Rhys Jones in their TV sketch show, *Alas Smith and Jones* (1984–1998).

Annie Get Your Gun (1950)

Director: George Sidney

Based on Irving Berlin's 1946 stage musical of the same name, *Annie Get Your Gun* provides a highly entertaining account of the exploits of the real life champion shooter, Annie Oakley. Packed with toe-tapping songs, such as "Anything You Can Do", and dazzling displays of marksmanship, this film is amongst only a handful of Westerns that revolve around the story of a woman. The message conveyed by the film, that "you can't get a man with a gun", is hardly a clarion call for feminists, and modern audiences may cringe to see Annie hide her light under a bushel so that she can win the heart of a proud man. Yet, even so, Annie is clearly the star of this show, which remains one of the most popular Western musicals of all time.

Storyline

Handsome ladies' man Frank Butler (Howard Keel) is the star of the world famous show, Buffalo Bill's Wild West. Arriving in Cincinnati, Frank challenges the townsfolk to a shooting contest. Local gal Annie Oakley (Betty Hutton) arrives and shoots a bird off a lady's hat. Realising that Annie is a wonderful shot, the local hotel owner enters her in the shooting match against Frank. Annie meets Frank and is instantly smitten: not knowing that he is her opponent, love-struck Annie asks Frank if he likes her, and is disappointed to discover that he favours elegantly dressed ladies over roughly attired girls like her. Annie wins the shooting contest and is invited to join the Wild West Show. Annie agrees, but has no idea what life

in show business entails. Attempting to explain, the showmen sing "There's No Business Like Show Business".

Gradually, Frank falls in love with the straight talking Annie. Discovering that their rival, Pawnee Bill's Far East Show, will be playing in close proximity to the Wild West show, Buffalo Bill

(Louis Calhern) asks Annie to perform a motorcycle stunt to lure the crowds away from Pawnee Bill. Thinking that this act will impress Frank, Annie agrees. The motorcyle trick is so amazing that Chief Sitting Bull (J. Carrol Naish) adopts Annie into the Sioux tribe. Jealous of Annie's celebrity, Frank, who had been planning to propose to her after show, runs off with Pawnee Bill's troupe.

In spite of having just completed a critically acclaimed tour of Europe, Buffalo Bill's Wild West show is bust, so the troupe decides to merge with Pawnee Bill's show, which they believe is solvent. Annie appears adorned with her shooting medals at the grand reception where the shows' merger is due to take place, but offers to sell her prized treasures when she learns that both shows are, in fact, broke. Frank and Annie meet, and declare their love for one another, but once again Frank's pride is hurt when Annie shows him her magnificent shooting medals. The merger and the wedding are instantly called off. Frank and Annie decide to have a shooting match to settle, once and for all, which of them is the best shot.

Prior to the match, Annie's friend Dolly (Benay Venuta) tampers with Annie's guns, hoping that by losing the contest Annie will win back her lover, but her plan is foiled by Sitting Bull. Taunting one another, Frank and Annie sing "Anything you can do, I can do better". Annie soon takes the lead in the shooting contest, but Sitting Bull persuades her to let Frank win, saying a girl "can't get a man with a gun". Annie realises that she would rather be married than be hailed as the best shot. Thinking he has won fairly and squarely, Frank is triumphant and asks Annie to be his wife. Annie joyfully accepts, and the way is clear for the two shows to merge.

Bullet points

- Judy Garland was originally cast in the title role but was forced to pull out on health grounds.

- In 1973 the film was withdrawn from distribution due to a dispute between Irving Berlin and MGM over music rights. The public was unable to see *Annie Get Your Gun* for almost 30 years.

- The film won an Academy Award for Best Music, Scoring of a Musical Picture.

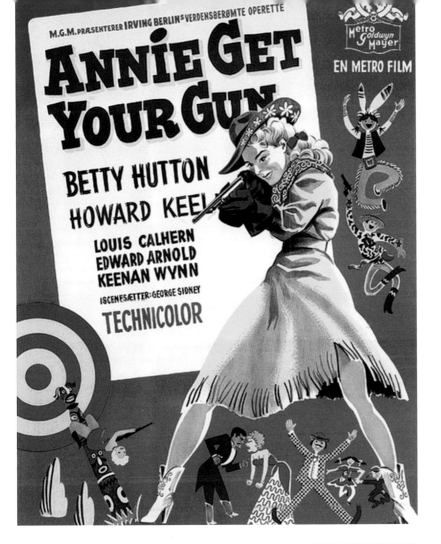

Bonanza
(TV series, 1959–1973)

Creator: David Dortort

Unlike over Western TV series, such as *Alias Smith and Jones,* the heroes of Bonanza do not fall foul of the law or find themselves in life or death situations on a regular basis. Instead, the drama revolves around the domestic life of Ben Cartwright and his three sons. Although a family based drama, *Bonanza* is notable for its lack of three-dimensional female characters, making it difficult for some female viewers to identify with the stories.

Storyline

The Cartwright family lives on a magnificent ranch, named the Ponderosa, near Lake Tahoe, Nevada. The family, which is headed by the thrice widowed Ben Cartwright (Lorne Greene), consists of Ben's three sons, each born to a different wife: Adam (Pernell Roberts) is a sophisticated architect who built the ranch house; Eric "Hoss" Cartwright (Dan Blocker) is a gentle bear of a man, and Joseph or "Little Joe" (Michael Landon) is the baby of the family. Other regular characters include the Sheriff Roy Coffee (Ray Teal) and his deputy Clem Foster (Bing Russell). A comic element is provided by the Cartwright's Chinese cook, Hop Sing (Victor Sen Yung), who regularly scolds the family for coming late to dinner. Through flashbacks we come to learn the history of Ben's three wives, and this endearing back-story adds even greater warmth to the family saga.

BONANZA

Bullet points

- "Bonanza" is a term used by miners to describe a large vein or deposit of ore.

- In 1962 country legend Johnny Cash recorded a full length vocal version of the *Bonanza* theme song.

Brokeback Mountain (2005)

Director: Ang Lee

Based on a short story by Annie Proulx, *Brokeback Mountain* is a poignant film that captures the tenderness of love between two men in the American West. The portrayal of this same-sex relationship is a major departure from to the traditional Wild West camaraderie depicted in films such as *Butch Cassidy and the Sundance Kid* or *My Darling Clementine*, and marks a coming of age for the Western genre. In 1894, Oscar Wilde's lover, Lord Alfred Douglas, wrote a poem that mentions 'the love that dare not speak its name'. In traditional Westerns, danger takes the form of Indians on the warpath, bandits and hired assassins, but in *Brokeback Mountain* it is this love, secret and enduring, that is most feared by the tragic heroes.

Storyline

In the summer of 1963, two young men, Ennis Del Mar (Heath Ledger) and Jack Twist (Jake Gyllenhaal), are hired by Joe Aguirre (Randy Quaid) to herd sheep on Brokeback Mountain, Wyoming. Ennis is an orphan who dreams of owning his own ranch, while Jack aspires to be a champion rodeo cowboy. Not afraid of hard work, the men defend the sheep from predators across difficult terrain. On a bitterly cold night the pair break Joe's rule that one man must sleep with the sheep while the other sleeps at the camp. Cuddling up together in the freezing tent, Jack tentatively touches Ennis, who gradually responds. Surrendering to their feelings for one another, Jack and Ennis grow increasingly close over the remainder of

the summer.

Summer ends and the men must part. Ennis marries his sweetheart Alma and fathers two daughters. Jack, meanwhile, struggles to restrain his feelings for other men. Working on the rodeo circuit, he

eventually meets and marries a Texan cowgirl, Lureen Newsome (Anne Hathaway) but struggles to fit in with her family. Longing for meaningful contact with another human being, Jack writes to Ennis in 1967, and they arrange to meet at Ennis' house in Wyoming: overcome with pent up desire, their passionate reunion kiss is observed by Alma. The friends arrange regular 'fishing trips' to Brokeback Mountain, and the distraught Alma files for divorce in 1975.

Hearing of the divorce, Jack suggests to Ennis that they fulfil Ennis' boyhood dream of running a ranch. Although tempted, Ennis declines saying that if they lived together they would be murdered by the locals for being "queers"; a fate that befell a neighbour when Ennis was a child. Sexually frustrated, Jack heads down to Mexico for sordid encounters with strangers in gay bars and clubs. In 1980, Ennis receives a postcard he send to Jack marked 'Deceased'. Contacting Lureen, Ennis discovers that Jack was killed when a tyre exploded, but Ennis imagines that he was beaten to death for being "queer"; a prospect that has haunted his imagination since childhood.

Lureen tells Ennis that Jack wanted his ashes to be scattered on Brokeback Mountain, so he visits Jack's childhood home. Jack's father (Peter McRobbie) refuses to hand over the ashes, but Jack's mother (Roberta Maxwell) is more tender, and invites Ennis to Jack's bedroom, where he discovers a shirt

that he thought he had lost back in the summer of 1963. Bloodstained from their brawl on Brokeback Mountain, his shirt is folded into Jack's own shirt from that summer: lovingly entwined they hang together on the same hanger.

The scene moves to 1983. Living alone, sick and poor, Ennis is visited by his eldest daughter, Alma Jr. (Kate Mara). Alma Jr tells her father that she is engaged to be married, and answers yes to her father's puzzling question as to whether her fiancé truly loves her. She leaves, and we see the shirts: they are still entwined but now Ennis' shirt is over Jack's. Beside them is a picture of Brokeback Mountain.

Bullet points

- *Brokeback Mountain* won three Academy Awards: Best Director, Best Adapted Screenplay, and Best Original Score.

- In 2006, the famous pair of entwined shirts sold on eBay for over a $100,000. The buyer, film historian and collector Tom Gregory, has described the shirts as "the ruby slippers of our time".

HEATH LEDGER
JAKE GYLLENHAAL
ANNE HATHAWAY
MICHELLE WILLIAMS

BROKEBACK MOUNTAIN

LOVE IS A FORCE OF NATURE

OWN THE 2-DISC COLLECTOR'S EDITION JAN. 23

FOCUS
FEATURES

Broken Arrow (1950)

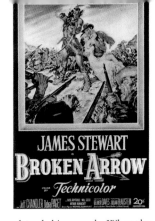

Director: Delmer Daves

*B*roken Arrow is based on the 1947 novel, *Blood Brother*, by Elliott Arnold. A fictionalised account of the peace agreement between the Apache leader Cochise and the U.S. Army, this film broke new ground by portraying Native Americans in a positive light. Instead of the pidgin English usually spoken by Indians in Westerns, the Apaches use conventional dialogue, which places the characters on an equal footing, and the various ceremonies depicted in the film are intended to demonstrate the Apaches' rich cultural heritage.

Storyline

*T*om Jeffords (James Stewart) comes across an Apache adolescent who has been shot and badly injured. A kindly man, he offers the boy water and tends his wounds. When the boy's tribe appears they are hostile to Jeffords but spare his life when they discover he has helped the boy. Some gold prospectors chance upon them and are viciously assaulted by the Apaches. Bound and gagged, Jeffords looks on helplessly. Released by the Apaches with a warning to stay out of their territory, Jeffords returns to Tuscon.

Jeffords' friend, Milt (Arthur Hunnicut) is in charge of the Tuscon mail service and is frustrated that the Apaches are killing his couriers and compromising his business. Jeffords volunteers to go to the stronghold of the Apaches' leader, Cochise (Jeff Chandler) to discuss this matter. In order to prepare for this mission, Jeffords learns the Apache language and how to make and read smoke signals, which he uses to gain an audience with Cochise. Persuaded by Jeffords' argument that the mail service is equivalent to smoke signals, Cochise agrees to stop attacking couriers who pass through Apache territory. During this visit, Jeffords falls in love with a beautiful young Apache girl, Sonseeahray (Debra Paget).

True to his word, Cochise guarantees the safety of the mail service, but some of his warriors attack an army wagon train and massacre its passengers. Seeing Jeffords as an Apache sympathiser, the townsfolk are about to lynch him when General Oliver Otis Howard (Basil Ruysdael) steps in and saves Jeffords. Known as the "Christian General", Howard wants to avoid further bloodshed and asks Jeffords to negotiate peace with Cochise. Cochise willingly agrees to the peace treaty, much to the disgust of a group of Apaches led by Geronimo (Jay Silverheels) who abscond. Although Cochise has instructed the Apaches not to attack the Butterfield stagecoach, the renegade Apaches ambush the coach as it stops by a river. Jeffords, who was accompanying the stagecoach, rides off to seek help from Cochise. Arriving with his warriors, Cochise rescues the stricken stagecoach.

Jeffords and Sonseeahray marry in an Apache ceremony, but their happiness is interrupted by the arrival of a rancher's son who has been escorted to the stronghold by two Apaches. The boy was found in the canyon armed with a rifle: Jeffords knows that the young man's father is a bigot who hates Indians, so he is sceptical of the boy's claim that he was looking for horses

stolen from him by Apaches. The boy says he can prove his story by showing them the horses' tracks, but when the Apaches enter the canyon they are ambushed by the boy's father and a posse from Tuscon. Jeffords is badly wounded and his beloved Sonseeahray is killed. Cochise manages to kill most of the posse, including the rancher who had initiated the attack.

Jeffords is heartbroken over the murder of his wife, but Cochise forbids him to retaliate. In a mirroring of Jeffords' discussion of the equivalence between the mail service and smoke signals, Cochise argues that the rancher's attack is equivalent to Geronimo's assault on the stagecoach. Peace, says Cochise, must be maintained for the sake of both sides. Acknowledging the wisdom of Cochise's words, Jeffords rides off, secure in the knowledge that wherever he goes, whether in cities or in mountains, his wife Sonseeahray will always be with him.

Bullet points

☛ *Broken Arrow* won a Golden Globe award for *Best Film Promoting International Understanding*.

☛ Members of the Fort Apache Indian Reservation played themselves in this film.

Butch Cassidy and the Sundance Kid (1969)

Director: William Goldman

Although a commercial success, *Butch Cassidy and the Sundance Kid* has been criticised for being uneven: while the characters' witty banter is generally admired, the chase scenes are considered by many to be too long. Quibbles aside, this film is great fun and inspired the popular TV series, *Alias Smith and Jones*.

Storyline

It is the late 1890s, Wyoming. Loveable rogue Butch Cassidy (Paul Newman) is leader of the Hole in the Wall Gang of thieves. Returning to his hideout with his best friend, the hotshot gun slinger "Sundance Kid" (Robert Redford), Butch makes the inglorious discovery that he has been usurped as leader by Harvey Logan (Ted Cassidy). Although he defeats Harvey in a knife fight over the gang's leadership, Butch decides to adopt Harvey's ill-fated plan to rob the Union Pacific Overland Flyer train on its outward and return trip.

The first train robbery goes well, and indeed the Fireman appears thrilled to meet the dashing Sundance. The marshal (Kenneth Mars) attempts to organise a posse to catch the Hole in the Wall Gang, but there is little support for this venture amongst the townsfolk, who appear to be in awe of the reprobates. Celebrating their success, Butch and Sundance visit the nearby saloon and Sundance spends the night with his lover, schoolteacher Etta Place (Katharine Ross).

The second train robbery does not go so well: having anticipated this assault, the President of the Railroad has reinforced

the safe and sent a second train down the line carrying a six-strong team of lawmen to capture the gang. Butch and Sundance hide in a brothel but are swiftly discovered by the posse, who appear to have super-human tracking ability and keep close behind the pair as they attempt to evade capture in a wood. The bewildered outlaws decide that the remorseless posse must include the celebrated Indian tracker, "Lord Baltimore" and relentless lawman Joe Lefors. Cornered, Butch and Sundance escape the posse by leaping from a cliff into a foaming river.

Butch and Sundance make their way back to Etta, who informs them that head of Union Pacific has instructed the posse to hunt and kill them. Realising that they will never be safe in the USA, Butch persuades Sundance and Etta to escape with him to Bolivia, which turns out to be a desolate place. Butch and Sundance make the humiliating discovery that they cannot rob banks here due to their ignorance of Spanish, so Etta sets about teaching them. Dressed as a man, Etta becomes their accomplice and together they become successful bank robbers: known as Los Bandidos Yanquis, their images are displayed far and wide on wanted posters.

Fearful that this celebrity will attract the attention of the dreaded Lefors, Butch and Sundance decide to go straight and become payroll guards for a mining company. Unfortunately they are ambushed on their first run and end up killing the bandits, whereupon Butch reveals that he has never shot anyone before. Thoroughly disillusioned with the straight life, Butch and Sundance decide to return to robbery, whereupon Etta, who cannot bear to see them die, returns to the USA.

Butch and Sundance rob a payroll mule train and head for lunch at a nearby restaurant. Recognising the brand on the mule, a boy alerts the Bolivian constabulary, who fire upon the pair. Butch and Sundance take cover in a building, but are wounded when they make a dash for ammunition. Not realising that they are surrounded by an entire regiment of the Bolivian cavalry, the grievously injured friends continue their banter, discussing the merits of a new life in Australia. With guns loaded, Butch and Sundance emerge from the building. The image freezes: we hear the gunshots, but do not see Butch and Sundance fall.

Bullet points

- The film won four Academy Awards: Best Cinematography; Best Original Score for a Motion Picture (not a Musical); Best Music, Song (Burt Bacharach and Hal David for "Raindrops Keep Fallin' On My Head"); and Best Writing, Story and Screenplay Based on Material Not Previously Published or Produced.

- "Raindrops Keep Fallin' On My Head" spent four weeks at the top of the US charts.

- In 2003, the film was selected for preservation in the United States National Film Registry by the Library of Congress as being 'culturally, historically, or aesthetically significant'.

ou never met
pair like Butch
nd The Kid

They're Taking Trains...
They're Taking Banks
And They're Taking
One Piece Of Baggage!

Century-Fox presents

AUL NEWMAN
OBERT REDFORD
ATHARINE ROSS

BUTCH CASSIDY AND THE SUNDANCE KID

A George Roy Hill - Paul Monash Production Co-Starring STROTHER MARTIN, JEFF COREY, HENRY JONES.
Executive Producer PAUL MONASH Produced by JOHN FOREMAN Directed by GEORGE ROY HILL Written by WILLIAM GOLDMAN
Music Composed and Conducted by BURT BACHARACH A NEWMAN-FOREMAN Presentation PANAVISION® COLOUR BY DE LUXE

Calamity Jane (1953)

Director: David Butler

Inspired by the success of *Annie Get Your Gun* (1950), this musical Western is loosely based on the true life story of frontierswoman and professional scout, Martha Jane Canary, better known as Calamity Jane. In contrast with the majority of Westerns, the central relationship in *Calamity Jane* is between two women, Calamity and Katie, but unfortunately much of the film's humour derives from the incongruity of a woman looking and acting like a man in the male-dominated Wild West, which may not sit comfortably with modern audiences.

Storyline

Calamity Jane (Doris Day) is a cheerful sharp shooter who likes nothing better than to guard the stagecoach against the Sioux and banter with her best friend, Wild Bill Hickok (Howard Keel), in their local saloon bar in Deadwood, South Dakota. Conscious of the lack of women in Deadwood, the saloon owner hires some actresses to entertain the men, but a near riot ensues when one of these 'ladies' transpires to be man in drag. Hoping to salvage this situation, Calamity Jane tells the disgruntled customers that she will travel to Chicago and bring the most beautiful woman of all, the singer Adelaid Adams (Gale Robbins), to perform in Deadwood.

Calamity travels to Chicago, where Adams is giving a farewell performance. Leaving for Europe, Adams offers her unwanted costumes to her maid, Katie Brown (Allyn McLerie), who puts on a dress and begins to sing. Stumbling upon this scene, Calamity assumes that Katie is

Adams, and offers to take her to Deadwood. Seizing this opportunity to fulfil her dream of being a singer, Katie agrees. However, on the Deadwood stage her nerves fail her: bursting into tears Katie admits that she is an imposter. Calamity asserts her authority to prevent a riot and the audience allows Katie to complete her performance.

Calamity and Katie become good friends, and with Katie's assistance Calamity begins to wear feminine clothes in the hope that she might win the heart of Lieutenant Danny Gilmartin (Philip Carey), with whom she is madly in love. Although Katie likes Danny, she tells him they cannot be together because it would hurt Calamity. The friends attend a ball, and Calamity is enraged by the sight of Katie kissing Danny: abandoning decorum she shoots the punch cup out of Katie's hand. Jealous and hurt by her friend's betrayal, Calamity confronts Katie in the saloon and orders her to get out of town. Undaunted, Katie borrows a gun and tells Calamity to hold up her glass, which she appears to shoot out of her hand. Publicly humiliated Calamity runs out of the saloon. Wild Bill tells Calamity that he shot the glass out of Katie's hand to teach Calamity a lesson. Calamity pours out her heart, saying she will never recover from

the loss of Danny, but when Wild Bill kisses her all thoughts of Danny are dispelled from her mind. Realising that she loves Wild Bill, Calamity's spirits are restored, and the next day she rides happily into town, only to discover that Katie, full of remorse over hurting Calamity, is departing for Chicago. Calamity chases after the stagecoach and tells Katie she is marrying Wild Bill. Friends again, the happy couples have a double wedding.

Bullet points

☞ *Calamity Jane* won the Academy Award for Best Original Song ("Secret Love").

☞ Although the film depicts the marriage of Calamity Jane and Wild Bill Hickok, there is no evidence that they were anything more than friends.

Colt.45 (1950)

Director: Edwin L. Martin

This film has all the ingredients of a classic Western: a gang of bandits; a gunfight on a stagecoach; a damsel in distress; Indians on the warpath, and a lone gunman out for revenge. But above all, it has the magnificent Colt.45, which is the true star of this highly entertaining Western.

Storyline

The Sheriff of Red Rock is impressed when gun salesman Steve Farrell (Randolph Scott) demonstrates the astonishing features of the new Colt .45 repeating pistol. Unfortunately for Farrell, his gun demonstration is interrupted by prisoner Brett (Zachary Scott), who grabs the pistols, shoots the sheriff and escapes, declaring that he is in league with Farrell.

The furious townspeople arrest the innocent gun salesman and throw him into jail. In what amounts to a bizarre sales pitch for Farrell's guns, Brett then stages a campaign of robberies and murders that showcase how regular guns are no match for the Colt. 45.

Eventually, Farrell is released from jail, but is infuriated when the new sheriff offers him a letter clearing him of all charges in return for information about Brett's whereabouts. Clearly, he must retrieve his Colt.45s from the murderous Brett to prove his innocence, and he sets off in hot pursuit across Texas.

Farrell comes across Walking Bear (Chief Thundercloud), the sole survivor of Brett's audacious attack on a band of Indians, who tells Farrell of Brett's plan to rob a stagecoach. Armed with his powerful Colt.45s, Farrell leaps onto the stagecoach and fights off an attack by Brett's gang. To his surprise, the sole occupant of the stagecoach, the beautiful Beth

Donovan (Ruth Roman), does not seem to appreciate his help. Farrell notices a white scarf hanging outside the stagecoach window as a signal to the bandits, and declares his intention to turn Beth over to the sheriff as an accomplice to Brett's gang, but is thwarted by her escape. Just as well, because Sheriff Harris (Alan Hale, Sr.) is in fact working with Brett and his gang!

Farrell makes his way to Bonanza Creek, and is duped into becoming Harris' deputy so that Brett can kill him. Thanks to Walking Bear and his fellow Indians, Farrell evades ambush. Beth discovers that her husband Paul Donovan (Lloyd Bridges) is in league with the evil Brett and denounces him, whereupon she is locked in a store room. Yet again the resourceful Beth escapes, and heads into town to inform on Paul, who shoots her. The shots are heard by Farrell, who takes Beth into his arms and rides off to get help from the Indians. Once Beth recovers she tells Farrell about Brett's plans to seize control of Bonanza Creek.

The Indians decide to go on the warpath, and imprison Farrell and Beth when they query this plan. Again Beth escapes and Farrell rides after her. The corrupt Sheriff Harris and members of Brett's gang capture Farrell, but the Indians come to his rescue. The injured Harris makes his way back to town to warn Brett. The wheel has, it seems, come full circle, and Brett is back in jail again, although this time he is playing jailer to Beth, who has once again been captured and is now Brett's hostage. When Farrell and the Indians arrive at the jail, the cowardly Brett uses Beth as a shield, but the Houdini-like Beth breaks away. Farrell enters the jail and sees that Brett is out of ammunition. He puts down his Colt.45s and the two men fight. During the struggle, Brett demonstrates inferior combat skills, and reaches for Farrell's Colt.45s, whereupon Farrell shoots him. Beth embraces Farrell, who has restored his good name and reclaimed his stolen Colt. 45s.

Bullet points

- This gun-obsessed Western romp was a huge hit, and inspired the TV series, *Colt .45* (also known as *The Colt Cousins*), which aired on ABC between October 1957 and September 1960.

- Its writer, Thomas W. Blackburn, also wrote the lyrics to *The Ballad of Davy Crockett*.

- The revolvers used in the movie were actually first model .44 Caliber Colts, not Colt.45s!

Cowboys & Aliens (2011)

Director: Jon Favreau

Based on Scott Mitchell Rosenberg's 2006 graphic novel of the same name, *Cowboys and Aliens* is a Western/sci-fi hybrid. Although this film is highly entertaining, it lacks the gravitas of the 2002 TV series *Firefly,* which arguably offers a more sophisticated blending of the Western and sci-fi genres. The film's title is a play on the familiar phrase 'Cowboys and Indians', and although Apaches are depicted sympathetically in the film, the film's subject matter might make us question the appropriateness of implying, even in jest, that the alien interlopers in the Wild West were the Native Americans, rather than the white settlers.

Storyline

It is 1873, New Mexico Territory. A man (Daniel Craig) wakes up in the desert with no memory of who he is, how he came to be there or why he is wearing a strange metal cuff on his wrist. He makes his way to town where is apprehended by Sheriff Taggart (Keith Carradine), who identifies him as Jake Lonergan, a wanted outlaw. Jake resists arrest, but is knocked unconscious by Ella Swenson (Olivia Wilde).

Taggart prepares to transport both Jake and a nuisance drunk, Percy Dolarhyde (Paul Dano) to Santa Fe for trial. A stand-off ensues when Percy's father, the cattleman Colonel Woodrow Dolarhyde (Harrison Ford) demands the release of both Percy and Jake, who has stolen Dolarhyde's gold. Alien spaceships appear and begin to capture the astonished townsfolk. The metal cuff on Jake's wrist opens and reveals itself to be a weapon: Jake shoots down a spaceship and the other ships flee. Realising that an alien has escaped from the wreckage, the townsfolk form a posse to track it down, while Jake heads to an abandoned cabin where he regains some of his memories. Jake remembers seeing the stolen gold and being told by a woman, Alice (Abigail Spencer) to return it, then being abducted by aliens.

Jake catches up with the posse and they come across an upside-down steamboat miles from water. They camp inside this incongruous item, which they surmise has been placed there by aliens, and during the night the injured alien kills one of the posse. Chaos ensues: most of the townsfolk flee, and those that remain are attacked by Jake's erstwhile gang, who are furious that he made off with the gold. The aliens launch another attack and capture Ella. Jake leaps onto the spaceship and attacks the alien pilot: the ship crashes and Ella is mortally injured.

The remaining members of the posse are captured by Chiricahua Apache Indians, who blame them for the alien attacks. When a Chiricahua warrior burns Ella's body she is resurrected and reveals that she has travelled from "beyond the stars" to save Earth from the same wicked predators that destroyed her own planet. Ella believes that Jake unconsciously knows the aliens' whereabouts, so he is given Apache medicine to recover his memory. Jake remembers that Alice was murdered by the aliens, but that he escaped, taking with him the

alien weapon that he wears upon his wrist, and most crucially he recalls the location of the aliens' operational headquarters.

The posse and Jake's criminal gang unite to attack the mother ship: Jake and Ella battle their way onboard and free the captives. Ella sacrifices herself to save humanity by entering the ship's core and destroying it using Jake's alien cuff. Jake is still a wanted man, but the sheriff and Dolarhyde decide to tell the authorities he was killed in the invasion. Jake declines Dolarhyde's offer to help rebuild the town, and rides away.

Bullet points

🖝 *Cowboys and Aliens* was shot using film, rather than digitally, to preserve the feel of a classic Western.

🖝 The film pays homage to the Western classic *Stagecoach* when Jake rides alongside a ravine and jumps down onto a spacecraft.

Dances with Wolves (1990)

Director: Kevin Costner

Dances with Wolves is based on the 1988 book of the same name by Michael Blake. With a running time of three hours, it is one of the longest Westerns ever made and features a spectacular scene involving bison that is unrivalled in its scale and majesty. To heighten the sense of authenticity, much of the dialogue is in Lakota Sioux with English subtitles, and music by John Barry intensifies this auditory experience. Costner was made an honourary member of the Sioux Nation in recognition of the cultural value of this masterpiece, which depicts with great poignancy a way of life that has vanished. The film ends with a lone wolf howling an elegy for the American frontier, and this film stands as a monument to the great horse culture of the plains, destroyed by white settlers.

Storyline

In 1863, wounded Union Army Officer Lieutenant John J. Dunbar (Kevin Costner) is told that he must have his leg amputated: preferring death he rides between the battle lines, thereby unwittingly distracting the enemy and inspiring his comrades who surge to victory. In thanks, Dunbar's leg is saved by a surgeon, and he is given his horse, Cisco, and his choice of posting. Wishing to see a vanishing world, Dunbar chooses the Western frontier, and is escorted to his post at Fort Sedgwick by Timmons (Robert Pastorelli). Alone in the deserted Fort, Dunbar befriends a wolf that he names Two Socks because of its white front paws. Timmons is murdered by Pawnee Indians on his way back to base, where the major has committed suicide, which means that the Union officers do not know of Dunbar's posting. Dunbar records in his journal his surprise that troops have not joined him at the Fort.

Human company eventually arrives in the form of Sioux Indians. Not realising that the Fort is occupied, Kicking Bird (Graham Greene) attempts to capture Cisco, but Dunbar forcefully objects. Tired of the ongoing attempts to steal his horse, Dunbar decides to visit the tribe's camp to reach an understanding. On his way, he encounters a grieving widow, Stands With A Fist (Mary McDonnell), the adopted white daughter of Kicking Bull, who was orphaned when the Pawnee tribe murdered her settler family. Stands With A Fist struggles to recall her native tongue, but manages to act as a translator for Dunbar, thereby helping him to develop a relationship with the Sioux. Enchanted by the Sioux's lifestyle, Dunbar is eventually accepted as an honourary member of the tribe when he helps them locate a herd of buffalo, and becomes a full member when he supplies the tribe with weapons from the Fort and helps them defeat a Pawnee raiding party. The tribe names Dunbar "Dances With Wolves" after seeing him play with Two Socks.

Dunbar marries Stands With A Fist and prepares to move with the tribe to its winter camp. Remembering that he has left behind his journal, which contains information about the Sioux that might endanger them, Dunbar goes back to the Fort, which is now occupied by Union troops. Mistaking Dunbar for an Indian due to his costume, the soldiers open fire and kill Cisco. Dunbar is captured and is assumed to be a deserter: Dunbar urges them to look at his journal, which contains the order for his posting to Fort Sedgwick, but it has been pocketed by a soldier. Led away for execution, Dunbar is followed by his loyal friend Two Socks, who is shot dead by the callous soldiers. Sioux warriors attack the convoy and rescue Dunbar. Realising that the Army will continue to search for him, Dunbar tells the tribe that he must leave for their sake. Although they plead with him to stay, Dunbar rides off with his wife.

Bullet points

- *Dances with Wolves* won seven Academy Awards including Best Picture.

- In 2007, *Dances with Wolves* was selected for preservation in the United States National Film Registry by the Library of Congress as being 'culturally, historically, or aesthetically significant'.

Davy Crockett (TV miniseries, 1954-1955)

Director: Norman Foster

With its catchy theme song, "The Ballad of Davy Crockett", this five-part children's miniseries was a huge hit for Disney, who went on to release a full length film version in 1955, *Davy Crockett, King of the Wild Frontier*. Playing fast and loose with history, *Davy Crockett* is a fun filled show in which the eponymous hero is embroiled in a series of unlikely adventures. Crockett was a real life hero of the Battle of the Alamo and sacrificed his life for his ideals, and it is therefore somewhat surprising to see him cavorting with his sidekick Russel in episodes that post-date the battle scene. Extreme deviation from the truth is, however, a common feature of Westerns based on real life characters, and arguably the popularity of the fictional Crockett

and his coonskin hat is testimony to the widespread acceptance of this approach.

Storyline

Wearing his jaunty coonskin hat, Davy Crockett (Fess Parker) and his friend George Russel (Buddy Ebsen) fight various battles under the command of Major General Andrew Jackson (Basil Ruysdael). Fearless Crockett performs valiant deeds, such as killing a bear armed only with a knife and suing for peace with Indians who have attacked a military outpost. Tragedy strikes when Crockett learns of the death of his wife Polly (Helene Stanley), but the plucky Crockett goes on to win a seat in the United States House of Representatives. Crockett and Russel make a trip to Texas, where they discover Mexico's General Antonio

Lopez de Santa Anna attacking the Alamo: this episode ends with the image of the flag of Texas, and Crockett's death is not shown. Crockett and Russel then go on to have a fur trapping adventure in Kentucky that culminates in a keelboat race to New Orleans, and in the final episode Crockett and Russel uncover a plot by river pirates to commit crimes disguised as Indians.

Bullet points

- Disney capitalised on the show's success by licensing the sale of Davy Crockett coonskin caps and other merchandise.

- Attempting to recreate the coonskin hat phenomenon, Disney featured a three-cornered hat with a foxtail in its miniseries, *The Swamp Fox*, but it failed to catch on.

Django Unchained (2012)

Director: Quentin Tarantino

Django, the 1966 Italian Western directed by Sergio Corbucci, was deemed so violent that it was refused a certificate in Britain until 1993. In his film *Django Unchained,* Tarantino blends this hyper-violence with the critique of racist ideology, also explored in his earlier film *Inglourious Basterds* (2009) in which anti-Semitic Nazis are scalped by U.S. soldiers in homage to the Wild West. Notoriously, Nazi Westerns were produced in the 1930s that tapped into the Nazis' eugenic theory, and this preoccupation with race is chillingly depicted by Leonardo DiCaprio, who plays the psychotic slave owner, Calvin Candie. In one of the film's darkest scenes, Candie displays the skull of one of his father's slaves and imagines that it explains why once race has enslaved another. In a clever inversion of Nazis ideology, Tarantino uses "Siegfried", the third opera from Wagner's *The Ring of the Nibelung,* to tell the story of a slave's quest to free his wife. The film's spectacular climax mirrors the ring of fire that Siegfried enters to retrieve his lover, Broomhilda: together they hail "light-bringing love, and laughing death". These words from Wagner, so admired by Hitler, are enacted by the lovers in *Django Unchained* and are thus re-appropriated to describe the liberation of African Americans. A visually stunning film with a powerful message, *Django Unchained* is one of the most original and thought provoking Westerns ever made.

Storyline

Texas, 1858. African men are being transported by slave traders when

they encounter a German bounty hunter, Dr. King Schultz (Christopher Waltz). Schultz is carrying a warrant for the arrest of the Brittle Brothers, and asks if he can buy one of the slaves, Django (Jamie Foxx), who knows the Brothers and can identify them for him. An altercation ensues, and the slavers are killed. Schultz offers Django his freedom in exchange for his help in tracking down the Brittle brothers.

Django tells Schultz of his enforced separation from his enslaved wife, Broomhilda (Kerry Washington). Intrigued, Schultz asks how she came by this name, and learns that Broomhilda was owned as a child by a German lady. Schultz tells Django the German folktale of Siegfried and Broomhilda, and says that as a German he is duty bound to help Django in his quest to liberate his Broomhilda. Django becomes Schulz's apprentice bounty hunter, and when Django collects his first bounty Schultz tells him to keep the man's Wanted poster as a good luck charm.

Schultz discovers that Broomhilda is now in the possession of Calvin Candie (Leonardo DiCaprio), the owner of the notorious Mississippi plantation known as Candyland, where slaves are forced to fight each other to death in wrestling matches called "Mandingo fights". Schultz is afraid that Candie will ask an enormous sum of money for Broomhilda if he knows that Django wants her, so he devises a plan to dupe Candie. Schultz pretends to be interested in purchasing a Mandingo fighter and Django disguises himself as a black slaver. Together they gain admission to Candyland, where Schultz secretly explains the plan to the delighted Broomhilda. Schultz feigns an attraction to Broomhilda and asks Candie to include her in the purchase of the Mandingo fighter: he will pay a small sum for the woman now, and pay for the fighter upon his return to Candyland.

The plan goes awry when Stephen (Samuel L. Jackson) notices loving glances between Django and Broomhilda, and suspects that the purchase of the Mandigo fighter is a ruse to get hold of Broomhilda. Stephen alerts Candie, who is enraged and forcibly extracts the full amount of money for the sale. After the paperwork is signed, Candie demands a formal handshake to close the deal. This is too much for Schultz, who despises the sadistic Candie, and he shoots Candie through the heart. A gunfight erupts and Django is captured.

Django is sold to a work as a slave in a mine, but escapes en route by tricking his guards: he shows them the Wanted poster from his first bounty and convinces the guards that this man is at Candyland, and that they will all become rich if they go back together and apprehend him. As soon as the guards release Django he kills them, steals their dynamite and heads back to Candyland. Django releases his imprisoned wife and then murders Candie's mourners when they return from his funeral. Django blows up the mansion with the dynamite, and rides off with Broomhilda.

Bullet points

- Christoph Waltz won his second Academy Award for Best Supporting Actor in *Django Unchained*. His first was for his role in *Inglourious Basterds* (2009), also directed by Tarantino.

- Tarantino won his second Academy Award for Best Original Screenplay for *Django Unchained*. His first was for co-writing *Pulp Fiction* (1994).

THE D IS SILENT. PAYBACK WON'T BE.
THE NEW FILM BY
QUENTIN TARANTINO
JAMIE FOXX
CHRISTOPH WALTZ
LEONARDO DiCAPRIO
KERRY WASHINGTON
and SAMUEL L. JACKSON
DJANGO
UNCHAINED
COMING SOON

Firefly (TV series, 2002)

Director: Joss Whedon

A spaceship soars over a herd of horses… This opening scene has been described by director Joss Whedon as his attempt to capture everything you need to understand about the series in five seconds. This cult TV series manages to fuse the genres of sci-fi and the Western while at the same time offering a hard-hitting critique of the gap between the rich and poor and the socio-cultural impact of globalisation. A multi-layered drama that is both dark and heart-warming, *Firefly* is a Western that explores what it means to live on the fringes of society and to rebuild a life after loss.

Storyline:

The year is 2517: the earth's superpowers, USA and China, have fused politically and culturally to form the Central Federal Government, known as the Alliance. The nine heroes of *Firefly*, who have fought on the losing side in a civil war, make a living on the fringes of society in an approximation of the Wild West. Their home is a Firefly-class spaceship named Serenity after the ill-fated Battle of Serenity Valley which marked the beginning of their exile.

The captain of the crew, Malcolm "Mal" Reynolds (Nathan Fillion) and his first mate Zoe Washburne (Gina Torres) are veteran "Browncoats" of the Unification War, a failed attempt by the outlying worlds to resist the Alliance's assertion of control. The crew makes a living through cargo runs or smuggling, an occupation made hazardous by the activities of the

Reavers, a nomadic group of human cannibals. The crew are joined by the fugitive siblings, River (Summer Glau) and Simon (Sean Maher). Alliance scientists have conducted experiments of the brain of child prodigy, River, resulting in schizophrenia, and her fractured sense of self is finally healed when the crew of Serenity accept her as one of their own. In a DVD commentary, Whedon claims that his intention is to depict how families are created, which brings to mind the fraught father-son relationship dramatised in the classic Western, *Red River* (1948).Consequently, much of the show's action revolves around the successful integration of the siblings into the Serenity 'family'.

Bullet points

- *Firefly* averaged 4.7 million viewers per episode, yet was cancelled after just eleven of the fourteen produced episodes were aired. *TV Guide* ranked *Firefly* #5 on their 2013 list of 60 shows that were "Cancelled Too Soon".

- Despite the series' relatively short life span, it received strong sales when it was released on DVD and has a large international fan base.

- The post-airing success of the show led Whedon and Universal Pictures to produce *Serenity* (2005), a film based on the series.

A Fistful of Dollars (1964)

Director: Sergio Leone

A Fistful of Dollars is the first "Spaghetti Western" by Italian director Sergio Leone. Its phenomenal success inspired the creation of *For a Few Dollars More* (1965) and *The Good, the Bad and the Ugly* (1966). Collectively, these films are known as the "Dollars Trilogy", and all three star the actor Clint Eastwood. *Fistful of Dollars* is a hard-edged Western that positions the lone gunman as a stylish and charismatic yet ultimately unknowable figure; a phenomenon summed up by the identification of the main character, played by Clint Eastwood, as the Man with No Name. Part of the appeal of *Fistful of Dollars* is the contrast between the dusty, barren surroundings and the mystique of the poncho-clad, cigar smoking stranger, and the funereal soundtrack by Ennio Morricone adds to the film's mournful aesthetic.

Storyline

A stranger, the Man with No Name (Clint Eastwood), arrives in the Mexican border town of San Miguel, where he learns that two families, the Rojos and the Baxters, are engaged in a bitter feud. Realising that he might be able to profit from this situation, the Man with No Name decides to stick around. His instinct proves correct when he observes the Rojo gang butchering a troop of Mexican soldiers and stealing their gold. Having taken two of the corpses to a nearby cemetery, the Man with No Name tells the Rojos and the Baxters that two men survived the ambush, whereupon both gangs dash to the cemetery to respectively silence the Mexicans and to get them to testify against their rivals. A fierce gunfight ensues, and the Rojos capture Sheriff John Baxter's (Wolfgang Lukschy) son, Antonio (Bruno Carotenuto).

While the rival gangs are fighting, the Man with No Name searches the Rojo hacienda for the Mexican gold, and is caught unawares by the beautiful captive Marisol (Marianne Koch). Realising that Marisol presents another opportunity to make money, the Man with No Name takes her to the Baxters, who arrange to offer her to the Rojos in return for Antonio.

Prior to the exchange, the inn keeper Silvanito (José Calvo) explains to the Man with No Name that Ramón Rojo (Gian Maria Volonté) took Marisol hostage after falsely accusing her husband of cheating at cards. During the exchange, Marisol's young son runs to embrace his mother, followed by her husband. Declaring that he had ordered Marisol's husband to leave town, Ramón instructs one of his men to kill him. Silvanito bravely raises a shotgun to protect the family, and is joined by the Man with No Name. Fearful of the stranger's prodigious gun skills, the Rojos back down. The Man with No Name tells

Marisol to go back to Ramón, but that night he secretly rides out to free Marisol. Reuniting Marisol with her family, he gives them money and tells them to flee.

The Rojos discover that the Man with No Name has freed Marisol, and subject him to a vicious assault from which he escapes badly injured. Believing that he is being protected by the Baxters, the furious Rojos torch the Baxter home, massacre the family and beat up Silvanito for aiding and abetting the stranger. The coffin maker, Piripero (Joseph Egger), smuggles the Man with No Name out of town in a casket to recuperate in a nearby cave.

Learning from Piripero that Silvanito has been captured, the Man with No Name returns to town, where he faces the Rojos in a dramatic showdown. Having concealed a steel chest-plate beneath his poncho, the Man with No Name urges Ramón to "aim for the heart" whereupon Ramón uses up his bullets vainly attempting to penetrate his chest. Having shot the rifle out of Ramón's hand and blasted away the other Rojos, the Man with No Name's pistol is almost empty. He challenges Ramón to reload his rifle faster than he reloads his pistol: with lightening speed he reloads and kills Ramón. Silvanito saves the Man with No Name by shooting dead a man who was aiming his rifle at him from a nearby building. Without ever having revealed his identity, the Man with No Name bids farewell to Silvanito and leaves town.

Bullet points

- The term "Spaghetti Western" was coined by the Italian journalist, Alfonso Sancha, to name a specific genre of Western produced and directed by Italians. They are also known as Italian Westerns.

- Sergio Leone originally intended Henry Fonda to play the Man with No Name but could not afford him, and eventually hired Eastwood, a relatively unknown actor from the Western TV series, *Rawhide*.

- Eastwood helped shape the image of the Man with No Name, providing black jeans, a hat and his trademark cigars.

- *Fistful of Dollars* is often compared with Akira Kurosawa's 1961 samurai film *Yojimbo*.

For a Few Dollars More (1965)

Director: Sergio Leone

For a Few Dollars More is the second film in Leone's celebrated "Dollars Trilogy", following *Fistful of Dollars* (1964) and preceding *The Good, the Bad and the Ugly* (1966). Eastwood repeats his stellar performance as an effortlessly stylish gunslinger in this tale with a twist: what looks like the pursuit of money is revealed to be a far more personal quest, and Lee Van Cleef's portrayal of brotherly devotion is outstanding. The moral of the story is clear: don't cross a man you can't outdraw.

Storyline

"Manco" (Eastwood) and Colonel Douglas Mortimer, the "Man in Black" (Lee Van Cleef), are two bounty hunters in pursuit of the notorious outlaw "El Indio" (Gian Maria Volonté) and his gang. El Indio is both brutal and bizarre: before engaging in showdowns he plays a musical pocket watch that he stole from a woman who killed herself while he raped her.

El Indio's next target is the Bank of El Paso, which contains almost one million dollars. Mortimer persuades Manco to infiltrate El Indio's gang, and he duly gains admittance by rescuing one of El Indio's friends from prison. Unable to open the bank's safe, the gang carry it off to the small border town of Agua Caliente, where Mortimer is waiting. Mortimer impresses El Indio by opening the safe without the use of explosives. El Indio tells his men that they must wait one month to receive their share of the money.

When Manco and Mortimer attempt to steal the money they are savagely beaten by El Indio's gang. El Indio instructs Nino (Mario Brega) to release Manco and Mortimer and sends his men after them, but Groggy (Luigi Pistilli) guesses this is a ploy to get rid of the gang, and he kills Nino. Groggy is about to kill El Indio too, until El Indio reveals that Mortimer has already stolen the money and hidden it. El Indio convinces Groggy to join forces with him to trap Manco and Mortimer.

The next morning, El Indio's gang confronts Manco and Mortimer, who kill them one by one. El Indio begins to play his musical pocket watch and is astonished to hear an identical watch playing the same tune. Mortimer and El Indio face off: the music ends and quick-on-the-draw Mortimer shoots El Indio dead. Mortimer takes El Indio's pocket watch and reveals that he is the brother of the woman who died being raped by El Indio. His revenge complete, Mortimer declines his share of the bounty for capturing El Indio and his gang, and rides off.

Bullet points

- Ennio Morricone composed the film's soundtrack, which was played on set during filming.

- The production designer Carlo Simi built the town of "El Paso" in the Almería desert. Known as *Mini Hollywood*, it is a popular tourist attraction.

Fort Apache (1948)

Director. John Ford

Fort Apache is the first film in director John Ford's critically acclaimed "cavalry trilogy", and was followed by "*She Wore a Yellow Ribbon* (1949) and *Rio Grande* (1950). All three of these Westerns star John Wayne as a military leader. Based on the 1947 short story, "Massacre", by J James Warner Bellah, *Fort Apache* is loosely based on an amalgamation of historical events. The short story is fleshed out by a romantic subplot featuring the former child star, Shirley Temple, but this romantic aside does not detract from the film's central exploration of leadership as an on-going process of negotiation that may break down with disastrous consequences. *Fort Apache* is the perfect illustration of the adage, "pride comes before a fall".

Storyline

The American Civil War has ended, and it is widely assumed that the honoured veteran Captain Kirby York (John Wayne) will replace the outgoing commander at Fort Apache. Instead, however, the command is given to the relatively inexperienced Lieutenant Colonel Owen Thursday (Henry Fonda), a widower with a daughter (Shirley Temple) whose engagement he thwarts due to class prejudice. Haughty and over-confident, Thursday ignores York's advice to discipline the corrupt Indian agent Silas Meacham (Grant Withers), whose actions are causing unrest on the Apache reservation. Thursday's poor judgement leads to an uprising amongst the Indians, and Thursday orders his regiment to charge into the hills in spite of York's warning that such a manoeuvre is suicidal. Furious over this challenge to his authority, Thursday dismisses York.

Thursday's regiment is all but annihilated and he himself is killed: a few soldiers manage to escape to York's position, and this group is spared by the Apaches' leader, Cochise (Miguel Inclan) as Cochise knows and likes York. Thursday's daughter is now free to marry the man she loves. News of the battle is carried far and wide and becomes known as "Thursday's Charge", recorded for posterity in an oil painting. Wishing to honour the memory of the dead, York does not reveal to the public that this assault on the Apache was a foolish mission led by a vainglorious man.

Bullet points

- The scenes involving the fort and the Indian agent's trading post were filmed at the Corriganville Movie Ranch, in what is now a regional park in the Simi Valley of Southern California.

- John Ford also directed Shirley Temple in the hugely successful adventure film, *Wee Willie Winkie* (1937).

Gunfight at the O.K. Corral (1957)

Director: John Sturges

Gunfight at the O.K. Corral is a fictionalised account of the Earp brothers' showdown with the Clantons in Tombstone, Arizona. In an earlier cinematic version of this story, *My Darling Clementine* (1946), Doc Holliday is a tragic figure who dies in the gunfight while in this film he is a more rambunctious character who lives to tell the tale, which is some indication of the extent to which history is freely interpreted in Westerns.

Storyline

It is the early 1880s, Fort Griffin, Texas. Ed Bailey (Lee Van Cleef) is looking for gunslinger John H. "Doc" Holliday (Kirk Douglas), who has murdered his brother. Meanwhile, Marshal Wyatt Earp (Burt Lancaster) has arrived in town hoping to apprehend Ike Clanton (Lyle Bettger) and Johnny Ringo (John Ireland), who have been released from custody by the sheriff. The vengeful Bailey is killed by Holliday in self-defense, whereupon Wyatt helps Holliday escape a lynch mob.

Moving on to Dodge City, Kansas, Wyatt discovers that Holliday and his sweetheart Kate Fisher (Jo Van Fleet) are also in town. Wyatt warns Holliday to stay out of trouble, but ironically he turns to Holliday when he is himself in trouble, and deputises him to help bring a murderous bank robber and his gang to justice. Johnny Ringo surfaces in Dodge City and challenges Holliday to a gunfight, which he declines, but he is later obliged to shoot the insistent Ringo in the arm. More drama ensues when Wyatt and Holliday thwart Shanghai Pierce's (Ted de Corsia) attack on a dancehall, and Wyatt falls in love with the beautiful gambler, Laura Denbow (Rhoda Fleming).

Wyatt and Holliday head to Tombstone, Arizona, after Virgil Earp (John Hudson) informs his brother that the notorious Clantons are trying to transport stolen cattle. Wyatt rides out to the Clanton ranch to inform them that he has legal authority to apprehend them, and the Clantons retaliate with an ambush that kills Wyatt's youngest brother, James Earp (Martin Milner).

Early the next morning Ike Clanton and some members of the Clanton gang engage in a showdown with the Earps at the O.K. Corral. Holliday is suffering from tuberculosis, yet volunteers to join the fight. An epic gunfight ensues: Wyatt's brothers Virgil and Morgan (DeForest Kelley) are wounded and Ike and all his men are killed. Victorious, Wyatt joins Holliday for a farewell drink before setting off to meet his beloved Laura in California.

Bullet points

- Lancaster and Douglas appeared in several more films together, including *I Walk Alone* (1948), *The Devil's Disciple* (1959), *Seven Days in May* (1964), and *Tough Guys* (1986).

- Sturges attempted to offer a more historically accurate version of this story in *Hour of the Gun* (1967).

High Noon (1952)

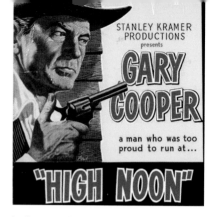

STANLEY KRAMER PRODUCTIONS presents GARY COOPER

a man who was too proud to run at...

"HIGH NOON"

Director: Fred Zinnemann

❛Do not forsake me oh my darling, on this our wedding day' – this haunting line from *High Noon's* theme song sets the tone for this award winning Western, which combines panoramic views with intense interior shots filmed in real time. In *High Noon*, the clock might be described as a character in its own right, and waiting for a train has never been more nerve wracking…

Storyline

The Marshal of Hadleyville, Will Kane (Gary Cooper), has married the gentle Quaker, Amy Fowler (Grace Kelly) and decided to settle down as a shopkeeper. Unfortunately for Miller, his resignation as marshal coincides with the discovery that the notorious Frank Miller (Ian MacDonald) is due to arrive in town on the noon train. Miller has sworn vengeance on Kane, the man who arrested him and caused him to endure the prospect of being hanged – a fate he has escaped due to a legal technicality. Miller's younger brother Ben (Sheb Wooley), Jack Colby (Lee Van Cleef), and Jim Pierce (Robert J. Wilke) are the menacing trio who form Miller's gang, and they are waiting for him at the station with brooding intent.

Clearly Kane is in danger and he therefore leaves town with his bride, but his sense of duty to protect the townsfolk from the evil Miller overtakes his sense of self-preservation, and he turns the wagon around. Amy is a pacifist who cannot be involved in bloodshed so delivers a warning on this, her wedding day: she will leave town on the noon train, with or without her husband. Undeterred, Kane reclaims his badge and begins a desperate search for volunteers to "greet" Miller, entering establishments associated with the dual aspects of the West: the bar, as a place of sin and debauchery, and the church, as a place of goodness and respectability. His efforts in both establishments are in vain: in one of the film's most powerful scenes Kane implores the church congregation he has so faithfully served as marshal to now serve him, to no avail. Many of the townsfolk want Kane to leave town to defuse the situation, and some even welcome the prospect of his demise.

As noon approaches, Kane is increasingly isolated: the judge who sentenced Miller is leaving and encourages Kane to do likewise. The elderly marshal who preceded Kane is supportive but is too frail to help and tells him to get out of town. Kane's abandonment is complete when his best friend Sam Fuller (Harry Morgan) makes his wife Mildred (Eve McVeagh) pretend that he is not home when Kane visits to ask for his help. The religious elements of the film bring to mind the words spoken by Christ at his crucifixion: 'My God, my God, why have you forsaken me?' (Matthew 27:46).

At high noon, Kane faces Miller and his gang alone. Kane guns down Miller's brother and Colby, but is wounded in the gunfight. Hearing the gunshots, Amy gets off the train and runs to help her husband. Compromising her religious beliefs, Amy shoots Pierce and is seized by Miller. Amy valiantly struggles with Miller, giving Kane a clear shot, and he shoots Miller dead. As the townsfolk emerge from their hiding places, Kane stares at the crowd in silence. Casting off his marshal's badge, which symbolises his commitment to uphold the values of a community that did not sufficiently cherish those values to help him defend them, Kane leaves town with his wife.

Bullet points:

- *High Noon* won four Academy Awards.

- Its writer, producer, and partner Carl Foreman was called before the House Un-American Activities Committee (HUAC) while he was writing the film as part of the notorious McCarthy trials, which inspired Marilyn Monroe's husband, Arthur Miller, to write *The Crucible* (1953), a play which condemned this "witch hunt".

- In 1989, *High Noon* was selected for preservation in the United States National Film Registry by the Library of Congress as being 'culturally, historically, or aesthetically significant'.

High Plains Drifter (1973)

Director: Clint Eastwood

As the saying goes, "vengeance is a dish best served cold", and you don't get much colder than the grave, from where the hero of this film arrives to punish both those who committed his murder and those who looked on. Like all great works of art, this film is open to multiple interpretations and we cannot truly identify the stranger, played by Eastwood. Although criticised by the great John Wayne as a freakish take on the classic Western, *High Plains Drifter* combines stock Western imagery with the surreal to great effect, and is widely acknowledged as one of Eastwood's finest films.

Storyline

A stranger (Clint Eastwood) rides into the mining town of Lago and shoots dead three louts who threaten him, thereby winning the respect of a dwarf named Mordecai (Billy Curtis). The sense of moral ambiguity intensifies when the stranger rapes CallieTravers (Mariana Hill) in retaliation for her taunts. Renting a room in the hotel, the stranger falls asleep and dreams about a man being savagely whipped.

The sheriff does not arrest the stranger for killing the three men: instead, the townsfolk offer to pay the mysterious gunslinger to defend them from Stacey Bridges (Geoffrey Lewis) and the brothers, Dan and Cole Carlin (Dan Vadis and Anthony James), who are about to be released from prison. Fearful they will come to town seeking revenge for being double-crossed over the murder of a man named Duncan, the townsfolk agree to offer the stranger anything he wants in return for their protection, whereupon the stranger appoints Mordecai both sheriff and mayor.

The stranger instructs the townsfolk to create picnic benches out of a barn, paint the whole town red, and write the word "hell" on the "Lago" sign, and he sets about training them in self-defense. These bizarre activities are accompanied by the unsettling revelation that Marshal Jim Duncan was whipped to death by Bridges and the Carlins while the people of Lago looked on. Duncan's death was desired by some of the townsfolk, fearful that he was about to shut down the mine. Telling the stranger of Duncan's murder, Sarah Belding (Verna Bloom) remarks that the dead cannot find rest in an unmarked grave.

The next morning the town is ready to greet Bridges and the Carlins with a welcome banner and picnic. Having positioned men on the rooftops, the stranger rides out of town. Bridges and the Carlins arrive and easily overcome the townsfolk's amateur resistance, and they corral the terrified people in a saloon and set fire to the town. Painted red and in flames, Lago is truly a vision of hell. In the darkness of night the stranger returns and kills the trio with gruesome means:

he whips Cole Carlin to death; hangs Dan Carlin with another whip and shoots Stacey Bridges.

The next morning the stranger rides off slowly past the cemetery, where he sees Mordecai carving a fresh grave marker. Realising that the stranger is departing, Mordecai remarks that he does not know his name, to which he receives the enigmatic reply, "Yes, you do". We then see the wooden marker, carved by Mordecai with the words "Marshal Jim Duncan. Rest in Peace". The mysterious stranger disappears from sight.

Bullet points

🖝 Duncan is the name of the murdered king in Shakespeare's play *Macbeth*.

🖝 Ernest Tidyman, who wrote the screenplay for *High Plain's Drifter* also wrote the award-winning screenplay for *The French Connection* (1971).

🖝 Two of the graves in the cemetery are marked "Sergio Leone" and "Don Siegel" in tribute to the two directors.

Johnny Guitar (1954)

Director: Nicholas Ray

Johnny Guitar is much admired by film makers: Japanese director Shinji Aoyama has identified *Johnny Guitar* as one of the greatest films of all time, and Spanish director Pedro Almodóvar pays homage to it in his film, *Women on the Verge of a Nervous Breakdown* (1988). *Johnny Guitar* is infamous for the off-screen fighting between the actors, some of whom vowed never the work with one another again, and its covert references to the oppressive McCarthy trials, which give this film a psychological intensity that has been likened to a nightmare. In a bizarre parallel of the plot, the lead actresses Joan Crawford and Mercedes McCambridge disliked each other, partly because Crawford had once dated McCambridge's husband, and Crawford allegedly resented the attention that the director Nicholas Ray paid to McCambridge, with whom he was supposedly having an affair. *Johnny Guitar* might be described as the evil twin to the other great Western about two women in a relationship compromised by jealously, *Calamity Jane* (1953). These films are united by wonderful music, but while *Calamity Jane* ends with the female rivals holding a double wedding with their beaux, *Johnny Guitar* ends with one woman murdering the other.

Storyline

Vienna (Joan Crawford) is a fierce talking saloon owner in a small Arizona cattle town who dresses in black and tolerates no nonsense. Vienna refuses to endorse the townsfolk's objections to the proposed railroad and further aggravates them by permitting her former lover, "The Dancin' Kid" (Scott Brady), and his friends to frequent her saloon. John McIvers (Ward Bond) is urged by cattle baron Emma Small (Mercedes McCambridge) to interrogate Vienna over the hold-up of a stagecoach, arguing that her friend the Dancin' Kid is more than likely to be the culprit. Emma wants to get hold of Vienna's land, but her primary motivation for wishing for Vienna to be run out of town is that she is jealous of Vienna, presumably because the Dancin' Kid did not return Emma's love and chose Vienna instead. The eye contact and brooding intensity of Emma when she is in Vienna's presence implies, however, that sexual desire for Vienna may be fuelling Emma's temper. A posse confronts Vienna, who is suddenly offered assistance by a mysterious stranger, Johnny Guitar (Sterling Hayden).

The guitar-toting, ex-gunslinger Johnny Guitar, whose real name is Johnny Logan, is another of Vienna's old flames, but it seems that the embers of this affair are still glowing, and indeed the heat intensifies until McIvers delivers an ultimatum to this most intriguing assembly of lovers: Vienna, Guitar and the Dancin' Kid have twenty-four hours to get out of town. Needing to finance this sudden departure, the Dancin'

Kid reverts to type and robs the bank with his gang so that they can travel to California. Their plan goes awry when they discover that their exit route is blocked by the chaos caused by the railroad crew's dynamite, and they are forced to take sanctuary in their secret hideout behind a waterfall.

The insanely jealous Emma convinces the gullible townsfolk that Vienna is involved in the bank robbery, and a posse ride to her saloon, where they discover a wounded member of the Dancin' Kid's gang, Turkey Ralston (Ben Cooper) hiding under a table. This discovery suggests that Vienna is indeed in cahoots with the Dancin' Kid, and in a frenzy of resentment and loathing the demented Emma persuades the posse to hang Vienna and Turkey and burn down the saloon. At the last moment Johnny Guitar arrives and saves Vienna.

Escaping the posse, Guitar and Vienna flee to the Dancin' Kid's hiding place behind the waterfall. The posse tracks them down and butchers the Dancin' Kid and his gang. The obsessive Emma challenges her rival, Vienna, to a showdown, and Vienna kills her. This death seems to break the spell of madness, and McIvers calls a halt to the killing: Vienna and Johnny leave to make a new life away from this demented community.

Bullet points

- ☛ Legend has it that Crawford, in a drunken rage, threw McCambridge's clothes into the street.

- ☛ Critics have described *Johnny Guitar* as a covert commentary on the McCarthy trials, comparable with playwright Arthur Miller's critique of the actions of the House Un-American Activities Committee (HUAC) in his play *The Crucible* (1953).

- ☛ *Johnny Guitar* was adapted into a stage musical, which debuted Off-Broadway in 2004.

- ☛ The title song, "Johnny Guitar", was written by Peggy Lee and Victor Young. Originally sung by Peggy Lee at the close of the film, it has been subsequently covered by many artists, and features in the 2010 game "Fallout: New Vegas".

- ☛ In 2008, *Johnny Guitar* was selected for preservation in the United States National Film Registry by the Library of Congress as being 'culturally, historically, or aesthetically significant'.

Kung Fu (TV series, 1972-1975)

Director: Jerry Thorpe

*K*ung Fu is an ingenious blend of Western and martial arts tropes: lawless communities terrorised by bandits; the taciturn man coming to the rescue; enigmatic words of wisdom, and the quest that must be fulfilled. Although it is impossible to say how many children signed up for martial arts lessons after watching *Kung Fu*, the number of us who longed to be as cool as Caine, the nomadic martial arts expert, must be legion.

Storyline

*I*t is the mid-nineteenth century, and Kwai Chang Caine (David Carradine) is the orphaned son of an American man and a Chinese woman. After his maternal grandfather's death he is accepted for training at a Shaolin Monastery, where he grows up to become a Shaolin priest and martial arts expert. Caine's blind mentor, Master Po (Keye Luke), is murdered by the Emperor's nephew, who is then killed by the furious Caine. With a price on his head, Caine flees China to the western United States in search of his half-brother, Danny Caine.

Carrying no weapon, Caine makes his hazardous journey through the Wild West armed only the skills he has acquired through practice in the monastery. Along the way he meets a preacher (played by real-life father John Carradine) and his mute sidekick Sunny Jim (played by brother Robert Carradine), then his grandfather (played by Dean Jagger). Caine is on a quest, yet cannot bear to ignore injustice, and in

each episode he steps in to defend the underdog, disarming lowlife cowboys with the flick of a hand and a well-aimed kick. As a result, Caine makes enemies and must live the life of a nomad, constantly moving forward to find his half-brother, and yet constantly reflecting back on his former life in the monastery. Through the use of flash-back scenes we see Caine as a boy learning enigmatic arts such as how to jump around on rice paper without tearing it, and without quite knowing how, or why, we are certain that this training means that Caine is invincible in the face of gun-toting bandits.

Bullet points

- The Shaolin Monastery which appeared in flashbacks was originally a set used for the 1967 film Camelot.

- The slow-motion effects for the action sequences were previously used in the 1969 Sam Peckinpah film *The Wild Bunch*.

- In her memoirs, Bruce Lee's widow, Linda Lee Cadwell, claims that Bruce Lee created the concept for the series.

Maverick (TV series, 1957-1962)

Creator: Roy Huggins

Maverick was a hugely popular TV series that employed an unusual format, with actors James Garner and Jack Kelly staring in alternate episodes as Texan cardsharp brothers, Bret and Bart Maverick. Blending gentle humour with fast-paced action, the show deviates from the Western archetype of the fearless, gun toting hero by depicting the brothers as fearful of being killed yet able to hold their own in a fist fight. In 1994 the film *Maverick* was released. Based on the TV series, it stars Mel Gibson in the role of Bret Maverick, while James Garner (who played Bret in the TV series) stars as lawman Marshal Zane Cooper. The film version of *Maverick* was a box-office success and is widely acknowledged to be as charming as the TV original.

Storyline

Maverick recounts the adventures of the handsome Texan brothers, Bret (James Garner) and Bart (Jack Kelly) Maverick, as they travel across the Wild West taking part in high-stakes poker games. The Mavericks are not gun slingers, and indeed claim to be among the slowest guns in the West, but are rarely beaten in a brawl. Combining a strong sense of ethics with a penchant for mischief, the Mavericks are likeable rogues who constantly find themselves in scrapes involving women and money. Incorrigible cardsharps who carry a $1,000 bill pinned to the inside of a coat in case of an emergency, the brothers never stay in one place for long and are often seen on Mississippi riverboats being gallant with a series of beautiful

DELL
Exciting
Adventure

SEPT.-OCT.
Still 10¢

Maverick

Bart Maverick
buys a guitar
and discovers

ladies. In spite of their self-professed appetite for money, when the Mavericks are confronted by a moral dilemma they always choose doing the right thing over making a profit, making this TV series one of the warmest-hearted Westerns ever made.

Bullet points

 When Garner resigned over a

contract dispute he was replaced by Roger Moore as cousin Beau, nephew of Beau "Pappy" Maverick; a role he played from 1960–1961. Moore went on to play James Bond from 1973 until 1985.

 During the height of the TV show's popularity, Dan Spiegle illustrated the *Maverick* comic book.

My Darling Clementine (1946)

Director: John Ford

Although this is a highly fictionalised account of the gunfight at the O.K. Corral, Ford's personal knowledge of folk legend Wyatt Earp gives this film an emotional intensity and sense of authenticity that is unrivalled. Cleverly incorporating a recitation of Shakespeare's *Hamlet,* Ford positions the notorious "Doc" Holliday (played by Victor Mature) as a tragic figure whose death is prefigured by the most famous farewell in literary history: 'Good night, sweet prince' (*Hamlet*, Act 5, scene 2). This film reveals the psychological agony that lies behind the coarse display of drunkenness and violence that features in so many Westerns, making this an all time classic.

Storyline

The year is 1882, and the four Earp brothers are driving cattle to California when they encounter Old Man Clanton (Walter Brennan) who tells them of a nearby town, ominously named Tombstone. Intrigued, the older brothers ride into Tombstone, leaving the youngest brother James (Don Garner) to watch over the cattle. They soon discover that Tombstone is a lawless place, tyrannised by a drunk who is shooting the townsfolk. Returning to their camp they make the even more unsettling discovery that James has been murdered and their cattle have been rustled.

Seeking to avenge his brother's murder, Wyatt (Henry Fonda) returns to Tombstone, where he takes up the vacant position of town marshal in order to hunt for his brother's killer. Tombstone is full of lively characters, such the consumptive doctor-turned gambler "Doc" Holliday (Victor Mature) and the dastardly cattle-obsessed Clanton gang. However, no one is more interesting than the charming Clementine Carter (Cathy Downs), who arrives in town in pursuit of her former lover, Doc Holliday, much to the annoyance of his mistress, Chihuahua (Linda Darnell).

The alcoholic Doc claims to have suffered a dark and mysterious transformation that renders him unworthy of Clementine, who then accepts Wyatt's invitation to dance with him, much to Doc's annoyance. Chihuahua is distraught when she sees Doc leaving town. Imaging that Doc has deserted her out of love for Clementine, Chihuahua flies into a jealous rage. At this moment, Wyatt notices that Chihuahua is wearing a pendant belonging to his murdered brother, James. Lying to conceal her indiscretion with one of the Clanton boys, Chihuahua claims that Doc gave her the pendant.

Wyatt, who had previously suspected that the Clanton gang had killed his brother, now threatens to arrest Doc for

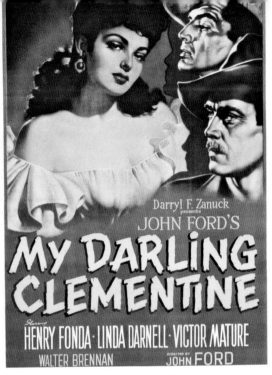

James' murder. Catching up with Doc, he forces him to confront Chihuahua and confess to his crime. Realising that she has implicated her lover, Chihuahua begins to explain how she received the pendent from Billy Clanton (John Ireland) who interrupts her confession by shooting her through a window.

Grievously injured, Chihuahua is operated upon by Doc, who is unable to save her. Meanwhile Virgil Earp (Tim Holt) chases Billy, who has been mortally wounded by Wyatt, to the Clanton ranch where he discovers Old Man Clanton (Walter Brennan) grieving over Billy's corpse. Old Man Clanton shoots Virgil dead, rides into town and dumps his body on the ground, crying out, "We'll be waiting for you Marshal, at the O.K. Corral".

Forlorn over the loss of Chihuahua, Doc volunteers to join the Earps on their dawn assault on the O.K. Corral. Wyatt informs the Clantons that he has warrants for their arrest, but they refuse to surrender and an epic gunfight commences. Suffering a coughing fit, Doc is shot and dies, but not before he kills the last remaining Clanton son. All four Clanton sons are now dead, and as his punishment, Wyatt tells Old Man Clanton that he has been left alive to suffer the pain of loss his family has inflicted on the Earps' father. Enraged, Old Man Clanton attempts to shoot Wyatt, and is shot dead by Morgan Earp (Ward Bond).

Wyatt and Morgan set off for California, taking their brothers' remains home to their father for burial. The lovely Clementine wishes Wyatt a fond farewell.

Bullet points

- Director John Ford claimed that when he was a prop boy in the early days of silent pictures, Earp would visit the sets and tell him about the gunfight at the O.K. Corral.

- The last silent film that Ford worked on, *Hangman's House* (1928), included the first credited screen appearance by John Wayne.

- Director Sam Peckinpah identified *My Darling Clementine* as his favourite Western, and paid homage to it in *The Wild Bunch* (1969).

- The title and theme song derive from the folk song 'Oh My Darling, Clementine'.

- In 1991, the film was deemed 'culturally, historically, or aesthetically significant' by the Library of Congress and selected for preservation in the United States National Film Registry.

Once Upon a Time in the West (1968)

Director: Sergio Leone

Widely acknowledged as a masterpiece, *Once Upon a Time in the West* pays homage to many other Westerns, and might be described as a love letter to the genre. For example, the opening scene of men waiting for a train is borrowed from *High Noon*; the funeral of the McBains is based on the funeral scene in *Shane* and the character of Jill McBain is inspired by Joan Crawford's depiction of Vienna in *Johnny Guitar*. In addition to powerful music by Ennio Morricone, this film makes use of intensified versions of everyday sounds and even silence to create a sense of foreboding. Leone broke with tradition by casting a lead actor, Henry Fonda, in the role of a villain, and in so doing took the genre forward while at the same time honouring its past.

Storyline

It is the Old West, and three gunmen are waiting for the arrival of a train. A harmonica-playing man (Charles Bronson) alights and asks for a man named Frank. The men tell the stranger that Frank sent them to meet him, and a gunfight ensues. The harmonica man is the sole survivor. Meanwhile, at Sweetwater farm Brett McBain (Frank Wolff) and his children are preparing to greet McBain's new wife when they are brutally murdered by a gang led by Frank (Henry Fonda).

McBain's bride Jill (Claudia Cardinale) alights from the train and is surprised to find no welcome party. She hires a carriage and stops en route at an inn. The sound of gunshots is followed by the entrance of a shackled outlaw, Cheyenne

(Jason Robards). We hear the sound of a harmonica playing, and Cheyenne names the stranger "Harmonica". Cheyenne's gang arrives wearing the same duster coats worn by Harmonica's assailants at the railway station. We discover that Cheyenne has been framed by Frank who has been paid by the railroad tycoon, Morton (Gabriele Ferzetti), to remove any impediments to the railroad he is laying.

Jill arrives at Sweetwater. Discovering that her husband has been murdered, Jill is about to leave when Cheyenne and his men arrive. Isolated and vulnerable, the former prostitute Jill surrenders to Cheyenne's desire. After he leaves she is anxious to be on her way, but is detained by the arrival of Harmonica, who insists she stays. Harmonica and Jill are attacked by two more of Frank's men, who are killed by Harmonica.

Jill is astonished when a large amount of building materials arrives at Sweetwater. Jill is captured by Frank and taken to the Navajo cliff, where Frank has a rendezvous with Morton. Arriving at Sweetwater, Cheyenne and his men are also baffled by the building supplies, but Harmonica understands: Sweetwater has a fresh water supply, and knowing

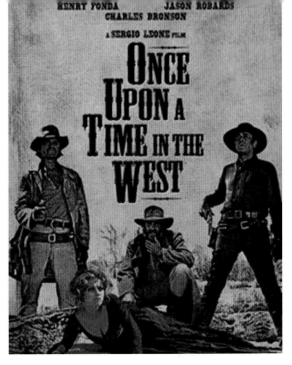

that trains need water to generate steam, McBain realised that the railway would also pass through Sweetwater and he had therefore secured the lucrative rights to build and operate the train depot.

Having seduced and intimidated Jill, Frank takes her to Flagstone to witness the auction of Sweetwater farm. Planning to buy it himself, Frank is outbid at the last moment by Harmonica, who hands over Cheyenne and uses his reward money to secure the purchase; a scheme contrived by the pair. Frank tries to buy Sweetwater from Harmonica for one silver dollar more than he paid for it, but Harmonica declines. Intrigued by the stranger, Frank asks who he is, but Harmonica refuses to say.

Cheyenne escapes from custody, and arrives at Sweetwater where building is well under way. Frank appears and confronts Harmonica, saying that the only thing that matters to him now is discovering what Harmonica wants. As Frank and Harmonica pull their weapons, their history is revealed through a flashback:

A younger version of Frank is watching a little boy balance his older brother on his shoulders. Frank forces a harmonica into the little boy's mouth, demanding that he play to entertain his sibling, who has a noose around his neck. Frank's men look on with glee, knowing that when the boy's legs give way his brother will be hanged from the church bell. Cursing Frank, the young man kicks his brother way and the harmonica falls from the boy's mouth as he collapses into the dirt.

Harmonica outdraws Frank who falls to the ground. Dying, he asks "Who are you?", and Harmonic replies by placing the harmonica into Frank's mouth.

Recalling the events of many years ago, Frank draws his last wheezing breath and the harmonica falls from his mouth.

Jill bids farewell to Harmonica and Cheyenne, who ride off together. Cheyenne falls from his horse, having been mortally wounded in a gunfight with Morton. Harmonica takes away his friend's body, and Jill takes water to the rail workers who have arrived at her station.

Bullet points

- The role of Harmonica was originally offered to Clint Eastwood, who turned it down.

- The music was written by composer Ennio Morricone, who wrote music for many of Leone's films. Leone played the music in the background on set to help the actors get into character.

- In 2009, the film was included in the United States' National Film Registry by the Library of Congress for being 'culturally, historically or aesthetically significant'.

Pale Rider (1985)

CLINT EASTWOOD
PALE RIDER (M)

Director: Clint Eastwood

Pale Rider pays homage to the classic Western *Shane* (1953), in which a mysterious stranger rides into town and saves a community. *Pale Rider* also shares similarities with Eastwood's 1973 film, *High Plains Drifter,* picking up its theme of the supernatural. However, while we are given clues to the stranger's identity in *High Plains Drifter*, the hero of *Pale Rider* is resolutely unknown. Filled with Biblical allusions and an apocalyptic finale, this Western is an epic depiction of divine retribution.

Storyline

It is sometime in the 1880s, and poor Californian miners are panning for gold when their camp is attacked and destroyed by louts employed by Coy LaHood (Richard Dysart). Jeering at their victims, the men shoot dead 14-year old Megan Wheeler's (Sydney Penny) pet dog, Lindsay. Megan buries her dog in the woods and implores God for a miracle, whereupon we see the image of a lone horseman on a pale horse (Clint Eastwood).

Megan's unofficial step-father, Hull Barret (Michael Moriarty), goes into town for supplies and is assaulted by LaHood's gang. The lone horseman rescues Barret, who invites him home in gratitude. While the stranger washes, Megan recites esoteric verse from the Bible about death being mounted on a pale horse, and Barret observes six bullet wounds on the stranger's back. The stranger appears wearing a white preacher's collar, and Megan smiles. From now on he is called Preacher.

Preacher helps Barret with the arduous task of moving a boulder that is blocking the river. LaHood's son Josh (Christopher Penn) wants to intimidate Preacher, so orders his powerful work hand, Club (Richard Kiel) to smash the rock. Undaunted by this display of strength, Preacher defends himself against Club's attack.

LaHood is concerned by these tales about Preacher: eager to get his hands on the canyon being mined by Barret and his friends, he had been hoping to intimidate the miners into forfeiting their claims, and fears that Preacher will strengthen their resolve to stay. LaHood therefore offers to buy the miners out at $1,000 per claim on condition that they leave within twenty-four hours. The miners are tempted, but Barret persuades them to fight for their right to stay.

The next morning Preacher has vanished, and Megan set off in pursuit of her hero. Megan is waylaid by Josh, who attempts to rape her in spite of Club's objections. Preacher arrives on horseback and shoots Josh through the hand, then takes Megan home.

Corrupt Marshal Stockburn (John Russell) arrives in town at the behest of LaHood. Accompanied by his men, Stockburn shoots dead one of the miners who had drunkenly taunted LaHood. Hearing about Preacher, Stockburn muses that he sounds like someone he once knew, but could not be, as that man is dead.

Preacher and Barret unite to blow up LaHood's strip mining site, but Preacher prevents Barret going any further with him by scaring off his horse. Riding into town alone, Preacher engages in a gunfight and kills LaHood's louts and Stockburn's men. Stockborn stares at Preacher in amazement, and says "You…" before he too is shot dead. Hiding in his office, LaHood aims a rifle at Preacher, but is shot by Barret who has arrived in time to save his friend.

Preacher rides off into the snowy mountains. Megan calls after him, "Preacher, Preacher we all love you Preacher. Thank you. Goodbye."

Bullet points

- The film's title is taken from The Book of Revelation (6:8) "And I looked, and behold a pale horse: and his name that sat on him was Death, and Hell followed with him".

- *Pale Rider* references a scene in *Shane* when two men bond over the pulling up of a tree stump: in *Pale Rider* Preacher and Barret attempt to remove a boulder. Both films end with a child calling out their love and farewell to the stranger as he departs.

Pat Garrett and Billy the Kid (1973)

Director: Sam Peckinpah

Pat Garrett and Billy the Kid is not held in such high regard as Peckinpah's earlier Western, *The Wild Bunch* (1969) and the production of this film was fraught with difficulties including influenza, alcoholism and in-fighting. Nevertheless, this film holds its place in cinematic history, with music provided by the legendry Bob Dylan and a first rate performance by country star Kris Kristofferson as Billy the Kid. Loosely based on the history of the Irish-American frontier outlaw, Billy the Kid, and his nemesis, the buffalo hunter-turned lawman, Pat Garrett, this film explores the appeal of the anti-hero. The ending references *Shane* (1953), but while the little boy in *Shane* is heartbroken by the departure of his hero and calls out loving words of farewell as Shane rides away, the little boy in *Pat Garrett and Billy the Kid* hurls stones at Garrett, who has killed the celebrated outlaw Billy, and Garrett rides off in disgrace.

Storyline

The year is 1881, and William H. Bonney, known as Billy the Kid (Kris Kristofferson), and his friends are mindlessly shooting chickens in Old Fort Sumner, New Mexico. They are joined by Billy's old friend, Pat Garrett (James Coburn) and Deputy Sheriff J.W. Bell (Matt Clark). Garrett tells Billy that he is about to become Sheriff of Lincoln County, and that he is duty bound to honour the residents' wishes to run Billy out of town.

True to his word, Garrett and his deputies appear a few days later and surround Billy's hideout. Men on both sides are killed, and Billy is arrested and sentenced to hang for the murder of Buckshot Roberts. While the gallows are being erected, Billy is physically and verbally assaulted by the mean spirited Deputy Sheriff Bob Ollinger (R.G. Armstrong). Ollinger works up thirst, and when he leaves to get a drink, Billy uses a gun that has been hidden for him in the outhouse to shoot Sheriff J.W. Bell in the back. Seizing Ollinger's shotgun, he loads it with coins and blasts him to death in the street saying, "Keep the change, Bob".

New Mexico's Governor, Lew Wallace (Jason Robards), introduces Garrett to members of the powerful and corrupt group of attorneys and land speculators known as the Santa Fe Ring, who offer Garrett $1,000 for the capture of Billy the Kid. Rejecting their offer, Garrett says he will bring him in of his own accord.

Billy returns to the farm at Fort Sumner, where he fights off three bounty hunters with the assistance of a stranger cryptically named Alias (Bob Dylan). Realising that Garrett is coming for them, Billy's friend Paco (Emilio Fernández) flees to Old Mexico and Billy follows him. Cattle baron John Chisum (Barry Sullivan) sends men to kill Billy: they shoot Paco, who dies in Billy's arms. Embittered, Billy returns to Fort Sumner.

Garrett and his men head to Billy's hideout and wait till sundown to launch

their attack. Billy is in bed with Maria (Rita Coolidge): hearing them make love, Garrett halts his approach to the house. Stepping outside, Billy sees the men: re-entering the house he encounters Garrett and smiles. Garrett shoots Billy dead, and then blasts his own reflection in a mirror. That night, Garrett keeps watch over Billy's body, and during this curious wake he refuses to allow anyone to touch the corpse.

The news of Billy's death travels fast, and the next morning curious townsfolk arrive to gawp at the notorious outlaw's body. Garrett rides off, and a small boy throws stones after him. Twenty-eight years later, Garrett is himself murdered by members of the Santa Fe Ring.

Bullet points

- 🖝 The role of Billy the kid is played by the country music legend, Kris Kristofferson, and his band members also feature in the film.

- 🖝 Bob Dylan was originally hired to write the film's title song, but ended up playing the role of Alias, and wrote one of his finest songs for the film, "Knockin' on Heaven's Door".

Rancho Notorious (1952)

Director: Fritz Lang

Based on the story, "Gunsight Whitman" by Silvia Richards, *Ranch Notorious* stars Marlene Dietrich as the gorgeous Altar who is rightly worshipped by the outlaws she accommodates in her den of iniquity, Chuck-a-Luck. Although dismissed as corny by some film critics upon its release in 1952, *Rancho Notorious* is a high spirited combination of the detective and Western genres, and Dietrich simply dazzles as the anti-hero turned heroine.

Storyline

Wyoming ranch hand Vern Haskell (Arthur Kennedy) sets out to avenge the murder of his fiancée Beth Forbes (Gloria Henry) who has been killed during an armed robbery of a store. Haskell, working first with a posse and then on his own, tracks down one of the villains, who has been mortally wounded by his partner in crime. With his dying breath the villain utters the words, "Chuck-a-Luck", and thereby gives a clue to his killer's identity.

A man tells Vern that a woman named Altar Keane (Marlene Dietrich) is connected with Chuck-a-Luck. Growing suspicious of Vern's intentions, the informant attacks him. Vern kills the man in self defense and is arrested for murder. Fortunately, the deputy is sympathetic towards Vern, as the man he killed is a wanted outlaw, and he tells Vern that he once knew a saloon singer named Altar.

Released from jail, Vern continues his investigation, and discovers that Altar left her job at the saloon after she won a

lot of money on its rigged chuck-a-luck game, aided and abetted by the gunslinger Frenchy Fairmont (Mel Ferrer), who is now in jail. Wanting to make Frenchy's acquaintance, Vern deliberately gets himself arrested, and together they break out of jail and head to Altar's horse ranch near the Mexican border, named Chuck-a-Luck after the source of her wealth. Vern soon discovers that this is no ordinary ranch, but is instead a hideout that may be hired by outlaws for 10% of their booty.

Altar is attracted to Vern, and when he notices that she is wearing a brooch belonging to his wife, Beth, he decides to capitalise upon this infatuation to discover who gave it to her. To maintain his cover, Vern takes part in a bank robbery, and is shot at by Kinch (Lloyd Gough). Vern presents Altar with her share of the stolen money, and Altar reveals that it was Kinch who gave her the brooch. Revealing his true identity as the vengeful husband of the murdered Beth, Vern declares his abhorrence for the life that Altar leads. Ashamed, Altar forsakes the life of crime and declares her intention to go straight.

The outlaws are not happy about Altar's sudden change of heart, and a gunfight breaks out between Vern and the outlaws. In spite of his jealously over Altar's feelings for Vern, Frenchy comes to Vern's assistance. Tragically, Altar is killed protecting Frenchy. Kinch dies, and Vern's quest is complete.

Bullet points

☞ *Rancho Notorious* was originally titled *The Legend of Chuck-a-Luck*, but the name was changed at the insistence of Howard Hughes, then head of RKO Pictures.

☞ Director Fritz Lang is best known for his masterpiece, *Metropolis* (1927).

☞ Lang fled Nazi Germany during the 1930s. Dietrich was already based in Hollywood at this time, and turned down the Nazis Party's invitation to return to Germany. A staunch anti-Nazi, Dietrich became a US citizen in 1939.

Rawhide (TV series, 1959-1966)

Executive producer: Ben Brady

The *Rawhide* theme song, complete with the sound of whips cracking, is best described as exhilarating. The compelling lyrics, "Keep movin', movin', movin', Though they're disapprovin', Keep them doggies movin' Rawhide!' set the rhythm for this fast paced show, which launched the career of actor Clint Eastwood. The show's hero, Gil Favor, played by Eric Fleming, is based on the real life trail boss, George C. Duffield, who recorded his experiences in a journal of 1866. Fantasy combines with reality in this hugely popular TV show, which contains many episodes about supernatural occurrences, yet the show never indulges in whimsy: many topical issues, such as racism and drug abuse are explored through tightly scripted stories. As the theme song says, "Rawhide. Yeah!"

Storyline

It is the 1860s, and cattle are being driven from San Antonio, Texas, along the Sedalia Trail to Sedalia, Missouri. Around twenty-five riders accompany the 3,000 head of cattle, worth over one million dollars in today's money, which are owned by about two hundred individuals. Trail boss Gilbert Favor (Eric Fleming), who is known as Gil for short, carries a large sum of cash to provide for all necessities along the way, so altogether the cattle drive is a sore temptation to thieves and rustlers.

Adventures occur along the trail when the drovers, including Gil Favor and Rowdy Yates (Clint Eastwood),

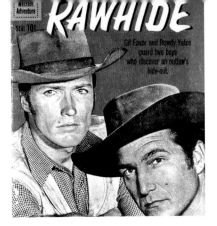

encounter colourful characters embroiled in a variety of problems which they help resolve. The younger and more rowdy characters, such as the aptly named Rowdy Yates, sometimes need to be rescued from trouble by their more mature and sensible companions, such as Gil. At various times the trail is attacked by Indians and cattle rustlers, and the heroes' lives are placed at significant risk. In addition to mortal concerns, the drovers encounter supernatural phenomena such as curses, a haunted Indian burial ground and a mysterious gypsy wagon.

Eventually the cattle drive reaches Sedalia and the cattle are sold. Celebrating with a drink, Gil announces his intention to retire from the business, and he sets off to Philadelphia to visit his daughters. The other drovers head back to San Antonio and embark on a new cattle drive. Reluctantly, Gil agrees to join them on what turns out to be an ill-fated mission. Wanting to beat another herd to town, Gil unwisely takes a shortcut near a cliff face: terrified by an electrical storm, the cattle stampedes over the cliffs and are all but lost. Unable to pay his drovers, Gil fears that his career is over. Rowdy Yates takes over as trail boss.

Bullet points

- Being cast as Rowdy Yates was the career break that set Clint Eastwood on his path to cinematic glory. Eastwood was not overly fond of the character of Rowdy Yates, finding him immature and clownish, and welcomed the opportunity to play a more serious role in Sergio Leone's landmark Western, *Fistful of Dollars* (1964).

- Frankie Lane recorded the song *Rawhide* used in the TV series. Written by Ned Washington and Dimitri Tiomkin, it has been covered by many other artists, including Liza Minnelli, The Jackson 5 and Johnny Cash.

Red River (1948)

Director: Howard Hawks

A long walk with a herd of cattle doesn't sound like much of a plot, but add in the simmering animosity and strangled love between the father–son characters played by John Wayne and Montgomery Clift and you have one of the most gripping Westerns of all time.

Storyline:

Thomas Dunson (John Wayne) dreams of setting up a cattle ranch in Texas, and presses on with his journey there with his trail hand, Nadine Groot (Walter Brennan), in spite of learning that his sweetheart back home has been killed by Indians. During the night, Dunson and Groot overhear a group of Indians planning to attack them. They kill the Indians, one of whom was wearing a bracelet which Dunson had presented to his sweetheart. The next day, an orphaned boy named Matthew Garth (played as a boy by Mickey Kuhn and as an adult by Montgomery Clift) wanders into Dunson and Groot's camp and is adopted by Dunson. The trio make their way to Texas, where Dunson establishes a ranch.

14 years later, Dunson is struggling financially so hires some extra men, including professional gunman, Cherry Valance (John Ireland), in order to drive his herd hundreds of miles north to Missouri, where he believes they will fetch a better price. The journey is beset by problems including a stampede and near starvation. Dunson's behaviour grows increasingly tyrannical, and his adopted son Matt finally rebels when Dunson attempts to lynch two men who had deserted the drive. With the

help of Valance and the other men, Matt takes control and elects to take the drive on a shorter route to Abilene, Kansas. He leaves behind the querulous Dunson, who vows to kill Matt.

On the way to Abilene, Matt and his men rescue a wagon train under attack from Indians, thereby saving Tess Millay (Joanne Dru), who falls in love with Matt. Matt gives Tess the bracelet given to him by Dunson, which had once belonged to Dunson's sweetheart. Matt leaves early the next morning, and some time later Tess encounters Dunson, who is hot on Matt's trail. Dunson recognises the bracelet and becomes emotional, telling Tess that all he has ever wanted is a son.

Matt reaches Abilene, thereby completing the first cattle drive along the celebrated "Chisholm Trail", and sells the cattle for a high price. The mood quickly darkens when Dunson arrives in Abilene with a posse to make good his promise to kill Matt. A furious fight ensues between Dunson and Matt, and Tess shoots into the air to attract the men's attention, urging them to acknowledge their love for one another. Tess's intercession is successful: Dunson tells Matt that he will honour his pledge to incorporate an M into the cattle brand, and he advises Matt to marry Tess.

Bullet points:

☞ The name Cherry Valance is used by S.E. Hinton in her coming-of-age novel, *The Outsiders* (1967) to name one of her female characters, Sherri "Cherry" Valance.

☞ John Wayne is the stage name of *Red River's* lead actor: his birth name was Marion Robert Morrison.

☞ In 1990, *Red River* was selected for preservation in the United States National Film Registry by the Library of Congress as being 'culturally, historically, or aesthetically significant'.

Rio Bravo (1959)

Director: Howard Hawks

Rio Bravo builds steadily from a relatively silent, dialogue-free start towards what is literally an explosive finale, and this trajectory is mirrored in its haunting theme music, "El Degüello", by Dimitri Tiomkin. Musicians Dean Martin and Ricky Nelson star in this film and their singing talents do not go to waste: at three points in the story they break into song, and their beautiful voices bring tonal variation to what is an otherwise harsh tale. A filmmaker's film, *Rio Bravo* has inspired other writers and directors to create variations on this story, and indeed Hawks himself was inspired by his own creation to make two more films covering similar material.

Storyline

Rio Bravo, Texas. Former sheriff's deputy, Dude (Dean Martin), once famous for his skill with a gun, is now a pitiful alcoholic with the derogatory nickname *Borrachón* meaning "drunk". Dude enters a saloon but cannot afford a drink, so Joe Burdette (Claude Akins) insolently tosses a silver dollar into a spittoon, which is kicked away by Sheriff John T. Chance (John Wayne). Humiliated, Dude lashes out at Chance, whereupon Joe punches Dude. In the heat of the moment Joe shoots dead an innocent bystander and is arrested for murder. Putting Joe in jail, Chance deputises Dude on condition that he remains sober, and tells his other deputy, Stumpy (Walter Brennan), to guard

Joe. Furious, Joe warns them that his powerful brother, the rancher and saloon owner Nathan Burdette (John Russell), will be angry about his treatment.

Pat Wheeler (Ward Bond) and the young gunslinger Colorado Ryan (Ricky Nelson) arrive in town with a wagon of goods. Hotel owner Carlos (Pedro Gonzalez-Gonzalez) warns Chance that his friend Wheeler is attracting unwanted attention by telling everyone that Chance needs help. Chance confronts Wheeler, who suggests that Colorado might look after him, but Colorado politely refuses. As Wheeler is walking back to the hotel, he is shot dead by one of Burdette's men. The startled Colorado belatedly offers to help Chance but is angrily rebuffed.

Chance and Dude locate the shooter and wound him, but he manages to escape into Nathan's saloon. In a repetition of the earlier encounter, a customer asks Dude if he would like a drink and tosses a silver dollar into a spittoon. Dude notices blood dripping into a beer glass from overhead, and quickly turns and kills the shooter. Returning to the hotel to rest, Chance

discovers that the mysterious poker-playing lady known as "Feathers" (Angie Dickinson) has been standing guard by his door. Chance advises her to leave town.

Nathan Burdette arrives in town with his men and demands to see his brother, Joe, but is sent on his way by the sharp shooting Dude. Feathers refuses get on the stagecoach and kisses Chance, whereupon he tells her that romance between them might be possible if only his current situation were less perilous. Feathers helps Dude and Chance when they are attacked by Burdette's men, and realising that Burdette will keep on attacking them, Chance decides to decamp to the fortress-like jail while they wait for the United States Marshal to come to collect Joe. Chance and Dude go to the hotel to pick up supplies, and the hotel owner and his wife are captured by Burdette's men, who hold Dude hostage and order Chance to release Joe.

Chance and Colorado are escorted to the jail by some of Burdette's men, who are shot at by the valiant Stumpy. Telling Stumpy to stay behind because of his bad leg, Chance and Colorado take Joe to a warehouse, where they have arranged to exchange him for Dude. During the exchange, Dude tackles Joe and a gunfight ensues. Stumpy, who has disobeyed orders, makes a fortuitous appearance and joins the battle. Dude overpowers Joe, and the altercation reaches a dramatic climax when Chance and Dude hurl sticks of dynamite at Burdette and his men, skilfully shooting the sticks to make them explode. In the face of this onslaught the villains surrender, and the film closes with a saucy embrace between Feathers and Chance.

Bullet points

- *Rio Bravo* is notable for its minimal use of close-up shots and the lack of dialogue during the long opening sequence.

- *Rio Bravo* inspired John Carpenter's 1976 film *Assault on Precinct 13*.

- Hawks made two further variations on the *Rio Bravo* story. *El Dorado* (1967) and *Rio Lobo* (1970).

Rio Grande (1950)

Director: John Ford

*R*io Grande is the third instalment of Ford's celebrated "cavalry trilogy", following *Fort Apache* (1948) and *She Wore a Yellow Ribbon* (1949). *Rio Grande* is based on a 1947 short story, "Mission With No Record" by James Warner Bellah, and the events it depicts resemble the real life expedition conducted by Colonel Ranald S. Mackenzie in 1873. *Rio Grande* was shot in just thirty-two days and is a testimony to Ford's legendry efficiency. In spite of being a commercial success, *Rio Grande* is not one of Ford's most highly regarded films, and its negative portrayal of the Apaches is perhaps distasteful to modern audiences.

Storyline

*I*t is 1879, and Lt. Col. Kirby Yorke (John Wayne) has been posted to the Texas frontier to defend settlers against the Apaches. Having raised concern over his lack of troops, Yorke is sent eighteen new recruits, including his son Trooper Jeff Yorke (Claude Jarman Jr.). Yorke has not seen his son in fifteen years, and is concerned that the other men might imagine that he is giving him special treatment. Consequently, Jeff is treated more harshly than the other recruits, but his stoicism wins him the respect of his fellow soldiers, and he is befriended by a pair of older recruits, Travis Tyree (Ben Johnson) and Daniel "Sandy" Boone (Harry Carey, Jr.).

Yorke's estranged wife, Kathleen (Maureen O'Hara), arrives and demands to take Jeff home because he is under-age, but Yorke refuses to release him. Jeff is keen to stay in the army, and points out to his mother that his discharge is not legitimate unless he and his commander both sign the necessary paperwork. Tension between Yorke and Kathleen runs deep, and has its origin in the Civil War, when Yorke was obliged to burn down his wife's beautiful plantation home in the Shenandoah Valley, ironically named Bridesdale. The man who lit the flames, Sgt. Quincannon (Victor McLaglen) still works with Yorke and his presence serves as a constant reminder to Kathleen of this devastating event.

Yorke's former Civil War commander, Philip Sheridan (J. Carrol Naish), is now the commanding general of Yorke's department, and he orders Yorke to cross the fabled Rio Grande into Mexico to confront the Apaches. Yorke is aware that if he fails to eradicate the Apaches he faces the prospect of being court-martialed for violating Mexico's status as a sovereign nation. Aware of this risk, Sheridan promises Yorke that the members of the court would be the men with whom he entered Shenandoah during the Civil War. Yorke accepts this mission, realising that this daring assault on the Apaches is an opportunity to restore his honour and unite his broken family.

Fearful of further Apache attacks on his fort, Yorke orders the evacuation of the women and children to the relative safety of Fort Bliss. On his way to Mexico with his troops, Yorke learns that the caravan has been attacked by the Apaches, who have abducted a wagon full of children and taken them across the Rio Grande to their camp in an abandoned Mexican village. The Apaches perform a night-time ritual of dancing and singing as a prelude to the children's slaughter. Yorke's mission to attack now becomes a mission to save, and he hurries his troops towards the village. Tyree, Boone and Jeff infiltrate the church where the children are being held, and Yorke then launches a full-scale cavalry attack and the children are rescued unharmed. Wounded in the attack, Yorke is carried back to the fort where he is given a loving welcome by Kathleen. In recognition of their valour, Tyree, Boone and Jeff are awarded medals.

Bullet points

- ☞ The film contains folk songs performed by the Sons of the Pioneers, one of whom is Ford's son-in-law, Ken Curtis.

- ☞ Maureen O'Hara stars with John Wayne in four other films: *The Quiet Man* (1952), *The Wings of Eagles* (1957), *McLintock!* (1963) and *Big Jake* (1971).

Shane (1953)

Director: George Stevens

We don't know who he is, or where he comes from, but we know that we like Shane (played by Alan Ladd), the enigmatic lone gunman who rides into town and out again, touching many lives and taking others. In a memorable scene, Shane and his new friend Joe (played by Van Heflin) pull up a tree stump, symbolizing their ability to join forces to overcome a foe. This scene is recreated by Clint Eastwood in his Western, *Pale Rider* (1985), when the men remove a rock from a river. *Shane* is notable for the poignant relationship between the gunman and the young boy Joey, to whom he confides his views on killing, saying "Joey, there's no living with a killing. There's no going back from it. Right or wrong, it's a brand, a

brand that sticks." This 'branding' is a theme explored in subsequent Westerns, most notably by Clint Eastwood in his masterpiece, *Unforgiven* (1992). For many, *Shane* is the greatest Western ever made and is unrivalled for the emotional intensity of its ending, which produced standing ovations in cinemas across the USA.

Storyline

It is Wyoming in the late 1880s. A buckskin-clad lone rider (Alan Ladd) makes his descent into a remote valley where he is spotted by an eight-year-old boy, Joey (Brandon de Wilde) who runs to tell his 'Pa' Joe (Van Heflin). Suspecting that the rider is a gunman, Joe is anxious for him to be on his way. This feeling is shared by Joey's mother,

Marian (Jean Arthur) who is strongly opposed to guns and is worried by her son's admiration for the softly spoken and enigmatic stranger.

At that moment, the cattle baron Rufus Ryker (Emile Meyer) and his men ride up to Joe's farm and trample over his gardens. Informing Joe that he needs more space to graze his cattle, Ryker says that Joe and the other homesteaders must clear out. The mysterious stranger, who is visibly armed, stands beside Joe and declares that he is a friend of the family, and Ryker and his men leave. Relieved, Joe and Marian invite the stranger to supper, and he reveals himself to be Shane. The whole family warms to Shane: Joe invites him to stay on with them; Marian casts him lingering glances and little Joey is openly infatuated.

Embracing his new life as a farm hand, Shane accompanies Joe and the other homesteaders into town to buy supplies and a soda pop for Joey. Shane is ridiculed by Ryker's men when he enters the bar and orders a child's drink. Instructed by Joe to stay out of trouble, Shane does not respond to these jibes, but during a subsequent taunting he snaps and ends up in a ferocious fist-fight, aided by Joe, much to the delight of the admiring Joey.

Joey asks Shane to teach him how to shoot, and Shane reveals his astonishing ability to draw his pistol with lightening speed and hit his target. Marian is displeased, and scolds Shane, saying that the whole valley would be a better place without firearms, yet her growing attraction to Shane is evident.

Seeking to intimidate the homesteaders into abandoning their farms, Ryker hires the mean looking gunslinger Jack Wilson (Jack Palance). Wilson provokes a fight with a homesteader and guns him down. Gathered around their friend's grave on Cemetery Hill, the homesteaders feel beaten and decide to quit their farms but are rallied by Joe, who persuades them that united they can defeat Ryker. Identifying Joe as the trouble-maker, Ryker hatches a plan to lure Joe to the saloon where Wilson can kill him. Warned by an insider of this trickery, Joe is determined to go regardless, knowing that Shane will care for Marian and Joey if he dies. Realising that this mission is suicidal, Shane tries to change Joe's mind, and knocks him unconscious when he will not listen to reason. Shane announces that he will confront Ryker himself, whereupon Marian begs him to stay, to no avail: Shane is determined to make this community safe for decent folk.

Shane walks into the saloon and goads Wilson using the same taunts that Wilson employed to enrage the innocent homesteader before shooting him dead. Wilson grins and follows suit, repeating the homesteader's last words, whereupon Shane pulls his pistol with astonishing speed and kills Wilson and then Ryker, who has drawn his weapon. Shane is about to leave when Joey, who has pursued his hero, shouts out to warn him that Ryker's brother Morgan (John Dierkes) is aiming to shoot him from the balcony. The rifle shot rings out and Shane fires back, killing Morgan.

Shane tells Joey that he is leaving, and to tell his mother that there "aren't any more guns in the valley". Joey touches Shane and blood runs onto his hands. Telling Joey not to worry about him but to grow up "strong and straight", Shane rides off, slumped and clearly injured, past Cemetery Hill and out of the valley, in a mirroring of his arrival.

Little Joey calls out plaintively, "Shane! Shane! Come back. Bye Shane."

Bullet points

- *Shane* is based on the 1949 novel of the same name by Jack Schaefer.

- It was one of the first films to use hidden wires to pull actors backwards when they had been shot from the front.

- *Shane* won an Academy Award for Best Cinematography, Colour.

- In 1993, *Shane* was selected for preservation in the United States National Film Registry by the Library of Congress as being 'culturally, historically, or aesthetically significant'.

She Wore a Yellow Ribbon (1949)

Director: John Ford

She Wore a Yellow Ribbon is the second film in John Ford's highly acclaimed "cavalry trilogy", preceded by *Fort Apache* (1948) and followed by *Rio Grande* (1950). *She Wore a Yellow Ribbon* was the most expensive Western ever made up until that time, and is famous for its expressive use of colour. Some scenes are very tender, for example when Capt. Nathan Brittles (John Wayne) waters flowers on his wife's grave at sunset, and this lightness is skilfully balanced by more brooding scenes, such as the magnificent thunderstorm that sweeps over the cavalry patrol as it rides across Monument Valley. Winton Hoch won the Academy Award for Best Cinematography, Color, and this film ranks as one of the most visually beautiful Westerns ever made.

Storyline

US Cavalry Capt. Nathan Cutting Brittles (John Wayne) has a favourite saying, ""Never apologize and never explain – it's a sign of weakness" and he lives his life by this maxim. On the verge of retirement at Fort Starke, Brittles is given one last mission: Cheyenne and Arapaho Indians have escaped from their reservation following Custer's defeat at the Battle of Little Big Horn, and Brittles and his cavalry troop must restore order and avert another Indian war.

This daunting mission is further complicated by the fact that Brittles must also deliver his commanding officer's wife and niece, Abby Allshard (Mildred Natwick) and Olivia Dandridge (Joanne Dru), to an eastbound stagecoach.

The lovely Miss Dandridge attracts the attention of troop officers 1st Lt. Flint Cohill (John Agar) and 2nd Lt. Ross Pennell (Harry Carey, Jr.), who compete for her affection. Miss Dandridge takes to wearing a yellow ribbon in her hair to signal she has a beau in the cavalry, but refuses to say who this lucky man is. Encumbered by the ladies and encountering fierce opposition from the Indians, Brittles fails both missions, and returns with his troop to Fort Starke to retire, "quitting the post and the Army".

Brittles' lieutenants continue to attempt to subdue the Indians, and deciding that he cannot bear to see more lives lost in this bloodbath, Brittles emerges from retirement and attempts to make peace with Chief Pony That Walks (Chief John Big Tree). When Brittles' peace mission fails he takes matters into his own hands. Risking death or serious injury, Brittles causes the Indians' horses to stampede, and this clever tactic forces the Indian warriors to return to their reservation. The indomitable Brittles is recalled to duty as Chief of Scouts with the rank of lieutenant-colonel, and there is widespread joy when Miss Dandridge and Lt. Cohill announce their engagement.

Bullet points

☞ The film takes its name from "She Wore a Yellow Ribbon", a popular US military song that is used to keep marching cadence.

☞ The role of Capt. Nathan Cutting Brittles was one of John Wayne's favourite performances.

Stagecoach (1939)

Director: John Ford

Stagecoach was the breakthrough film for legendry Western actor, John Wayne. Based on the 1937 short story by Ernest Haycox, "The Stage to Lordsburg", *Stagecoach* might be described as a morality play. Nine individuals, some of whom are morally upright, such as the officer's wife, and some of whom are morally dubious, such as the saloon girl, are brought together on a journey that might be likened to the pilgrimage described in Geoffrey Chaucer's medieval masterpiece, *The Canterbury Tales*. Through intense interaction in the confines of a stagecoach, these characters are forced to confront their prejudices and learn to pull together in order to survive, and the conclusion of *Stagecoach* ranks as one of the happiest Western film endings of all time.

Storyline

It is 1880 and an urgent telegram arrives containing just one word, "Geronimo". The telegraph line goes dead but the message is clear: Apache warriors led by the fearsome Geronimo are on the warpath, and no one on the border between Arizona and Mexico is safe. In the little town on Tonto, Arizona, a group of strangers prepares to board the stagecoach to Lordsburg, New Mexico. The dashing Lieutenant Blanchard (Tim Holt) warns the group that they may come under attack by Geronimo's Apache warriors and that a cavalry detachment of troops will therefore accompany the stagecoach. The ladies and gentlemen are determined to risk this journey, even though it passes directly through Apache territory,

Above:
*Stagecoach was
the first of many
westerns Ford
shot at Monument
Valley*

as each of them is compelled to leave Tonto. The beautiful saloon girl Dallas (Claire Trevor) is being driven out of town by the spiteful members of the "Law and Order League"; Doc Boone (Thomas Mitchell) is an alcoholic doctor who is being evicted for not paying his rent; Lucy Mallory (Louise Platt) is the pregnant wife of a cavalry officer and is travelling to see him; Samuel Peacock (Donald Meek) is a whiskey salesman who must move from town to town to make his living.

Marshal Curly Wilcox (George Bancroft) informs the stage driver that his normal shotgun guard has gone searching for the fugitive, Ringo Kid (John Wayne),

who has vowed to avenge the death of his father and brother at the hands of Luke Plummer (Tom Tyler). Curly says he will take the shotgun guard's place and ride with them to Lordsburg. Not long after they depart, the stagecoach picks up two more passengers, the Southern gentleman Hatfield (John Carradine), and the banker Gatewood (Berton Churchill) who has embezzled the Wells Fargo payroll.

The stagecoach comes across Curly's friend, the Ringo Kid. In spite of their friendship, Curly is obliged to take Ringo into custody. Sitting on the floor of the cramped stagecoach, Ringo takes a liking to Dallas, who is being shunned by the other passengers as a lady of ill repute.

Reaching the way station at Dry Fork, the group makes the unsettling discovery that the expected cavalry detachment has been summoned to Apache Wells. The group takes a vote, and decides to press onwards unguarded, rather than go back.

Mrs Mallory discovers that her husband has been injured in battle and goes into labour. Doc Boone and Dallas help deliver her daughter, and impressed by her kindness, Ringo asks Dallas to marry him. Seeing Apache smoke signals, the passengers quickly depart for Lee's Ferry, only to discover that it has been destroyed by the Apaches. Curly decides to float the stagecoach across the river to safety, but on the other side they are attacked by Apache warriors. Some of the passengers are injured and they run out of ammunition. Just as Hatfield is about to use his last bullet to prevent Mrs Mallory from being taken alive, he is fatally wounded. When all appears to be lost, the 6th US cavalry rides to their rescue.

The stagecoach eventually arrives in Lordsburg, and Gatewood is promptly arrested for embezzlement. Mrs Mallory learns that her husband is not seriously injured, and kind-hearted Dallas gives her a shawl to show that she does not resent Mrs Mallory's previous cold treatment

of her. Although Dallas has begged Ringo not to confront the Plummers, he is determined to avenge his father and brother, and Curly lets him go. Ringo emerges from the shootout victorious: expecting to go straight to jail, he tells Curly to take Dallas to his ranch in Mexico where she will have a comfortable home. Curly, however, has other plans: instead of arresting Ringo, he arranges for Dallas to join him on a wagon out of town.

Bullet points

- *Stagecoach* was the first of many Westerns that Ford shot on location in Monument Valley.

- Orson Welles described *Stagecoach* as a perfect textbook of film making and claimed to have watched it more than 40 times during the making of *Citizen Kane*.

- In 1995, *Stagecoach* was deemed 'culturally, historically, or aesthetically significant' by the United States Library of Congress and selected for preservation in their National Film Registry.

The Alamo (1960)

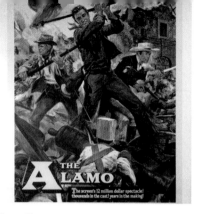

THE ALAMO

The screen's 12 million dollar spectacle! thousands in the cast! years in the making!

Director: John Wayne

The Alamo is loosely based on the historic 1836 Battle of the Alamo. Actor and director John Wayne was passionate about this film, which expresses his political views. In one scene, the character played by Wayne says, "Republic. I like the sound of the word. Means that people can live free, talk free, go or come, buy or sell, be drunk or sober, however they choose". Wayne was unsympathetic to left-wing opponents of the McCarthy trials, which attempted to root out communists in the USA, and *The Alamo* is a symbolic refutation of the imposition of un-American ideals. Although not considered to be amongst the finest Westerns, *The Alamo* is sure to quicken the pulse of freedom lovers everywhere.

Storyline

It is 1836, and Mexican General Antonio López de Santa Anna (Ruben Padilla) and his army have arrived at San Antonio to suppress a frontier rebellion during the Texas Revolution. The rebels, led by Lieutenant Colonel William Travis (Laurence Harvey), have retreated to an old fortified mission known as the Alamo. Under siege, Travis has put out a call for help and legendary knife-fighter Jim Bowie (Richard Widmark) has arrived with reinforcements. Hundreds of civilians volunteer to defend the Alamo, including the frontiersman-turned Tennessee congressman, Col. Davy Crockett (John Wayne).

Travis is enraged when Bowie goes to Santa Anna under the peace flag, saying he will only negotiate peace from a position of power. The Texans conduct a daring night time raid in which they sabotage the Mexicans' biggest cannon. Their confidence raised, the Texans believe that the strong force led by Colonel James Fannin is on its way to break the siege. Crockett, however, is not convinced as his gut instinct tells him they are in imminent danger. Crockett sends his young friend from Tennessee, Smitty (Frankie Avalon), to ask the leader of the Texas army, General Sam Houston (Richard Boone) for help, in the hope that by leaving Smitty's life will be saved.

The Mexicans attack the Alamo and Texan morale falters when Travis informs his men that Fannin's reinforcements have been ambushed by the Mexicans, who have viciously slaughtered the troops after they surrendered. Realising that the defence of the Alamo is now a suicide mission, Travis vows to fight on, but tells his men they are free to leave. Heroically, Crockett, Bowie and their men choose honour over life and pledge to fight till the end.

On the thirteenth day of the siege, a Mexican artillery bombardment blasts a hole in the wall of the Alamo, and Mexican troops surge into the building. Although the besieged Texans manage to kill hundreds of Mexicans, they are soon overwhelmed by Santa Anna's forces. Travis is shot and killed, and the Texans retreat to their final position. Crockett dies heroically, a lance through his side, as he ignites explosives. Bowie is bayoneted and dies fighting till his last breath. The battle is over, and the Alamo has fallen to the Mexicans.

Smitty returns, but he is too late. Seeing the carnage from a distance, he removes his hat as a mark of respect to the heroes of the Alamo.

Bullet points

- The movie set, dubbed Alamo Village, was constructed near Brackettville, Texas, on the ranch of James T. Shahan. Taking more than two years to construct, the set has been used in more than a hundred subsequent Westerns.

- Dimitri Tiomkin composed the film's score, including the song "The Green Leaves of Summer".

- *The Alamo* won the Academy Award for Best Sound (Gordon E. Sawyer, Fred Hynes).

The Good, the Bad and the Ugly (1966)

Director: Sergio Leone

*T*he Good, the Bad and the Ugly is the third film in Leone's highly acclaimed Dollars Trilogy, preceded by *Fistful of Dollars* (1964) and *For a Few Dollars More* (1965). Although this is the last film in the series, the events take place during the American Civil War, making it is the predecessor to the narratives in the other two films. Condemned by some as overly violent, *The Good, the Bad and the Ugly* was a commercial success, and the title has become an idiom used to describe the complete embrace of things, similar to the idiom "warts and all".

Storyline

*T*he American Civil War is raging, and bounty hunters enter a Western ghost town seeking to capture "Ugly" Mexican bandit, Tuco Ramirez (Eli Wallach). Meanwhile, the "Bad" mercenary, Angel Eyes (Lee Van Cleef), interrogates a man about the fugitive Jackson (Antonio Casale), who is now calling himself Bill Carson and has information about a cache of Confederate gold.

Tuco is ambushed by yet more bounty hunters keen to collect his reward money, but they are gunned down by the "Good" bounty hunter, Blondie (Clint Eastwood). Blondie delivers Tuco to the authorities and collects the $2,000 reward. Just as Tuco is about to be hanged, Blondie frees him by shooting through the hangman's rope and they escape together. Growing tired of Tuco's complaints about how the money has been split, Blondie abandons him in the desert.

Tuco pursues and captures Blondie and exacts his revenge by forcing him to walk across the desert. Suffering from heat exhaustion, Blondie collapses. Just as Tuco is about to shoot Blondie, a runaway carriage appears containing the mortally injured Bill Carson, who tells them that $200,000 of looted Confederate gold is buried in a grave in Sad Hill Cemetery. Carson faints, and Tuco goes to fetch some water. When Tuco returns, he finds Carson dead. Blondie tells Tuco that Carson told him the name on the grave containing the gold. Realising that he needs Blondie in order to retrieve the gold, Tuco spares his life.

Disguised as Confederate soldiers, Tuco and Blondie set off on their quest for the gold, but are promptly captured by Union soldiers and taken to a prison camp. At roll call, Tuco says his name is Bill Carson: Angel Eyes has disguised himself as a Union sergeant and immediately summons Tuco for torture, demanding that he reveal the location of the gold. Tuco tells Angel Eyes the name of the cemetery, but says that only Blondie knows the name on the grave. Having surmised that Blondie is unlikely to yield to torture, Angel Eyes offers Blondie an equal share of the gold in exchange for

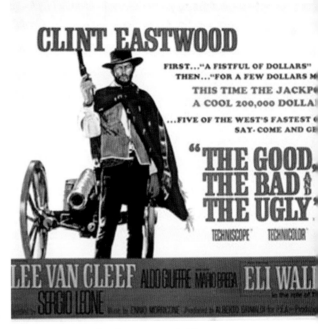

his information. Blondie agrees and rides out with Angel Eyes and his gang. Tuco is loaded into a Union prison train, but manages to escape.

Blondie, Angel Eyes and his gang arrive in the evacuated town, followed by Tuco. Blondie and Tuco covertly renew their partnership and make their way around the wrecked town picking off Angel Eyes' men, but the man himself has escaped. Blondie and Tuco head for the cemetery and are once again captured by Union troops who occupy once side of a bridge: the Confederate army and the cemetery are on the other side. Desperate to get to the cemetery, Tuco and Blondie enlist in the Union army and hatch a plan to disperse both armies by blowing up the bridge. Just before detonation, Tuco reveals the name of the cemetery and Blondie reveals the name of the grave, "Arch Stanton". The explosion provokes a fierce artillery battle and by morning both sides are gone.

The treacherous Tuco steals a horse and sets off without Blondie: searching long and hard he eventually locates Stanton's grave and begins to dig. Blondie arrives and aims a gun at Tuco, telling him to keep digging. Angel Eyes suddenly appears and aims a gun at both of them. Blondie kicks open Stanton's grave, which contains nothing more than bones. Scrawling the real grave's name on a stone, Blondie challenges Tuco and Angel Eyes to a three-way duel. Blondie is faster than Angel Eyes, and shoots him dead. Discovering that Blondie unloaded his gun the night before, Tuco is obliged to walk at gunpoint to a grave marked "Unknown".

Blondie orders Tuco to dig, and Tuco is elated to find sacks of gold. This joy is short lived: looking up, Tuco sees a hangman's noose. Blondie forces Tuco to stand on top of a grave marker then puts the noose around his neck. Leaving Tuco's share of the gold, Blondie bids farewell and rides off. Tuco curses Blondie, who stops in the distance: with his rifle Blondie fires a single shot that severs the rope, in a mirroring of the previous liberation of Tuco. Tuco is dumped unceremoniously onto his share of the gold. Blondie smiles and rides off as Tuco continues to curse his friend.

Bullet points

- Ennio Morricone composed the famous film score, including the main theme that mimics the howl of a coyote.

- The design for the cemetery was based on an ancient Roman arena.

- The blowing up of the bridge was filmed twice, as the first attempt destroyed all of the cameras.

The Magnificent Seven (1960)

Director: John Sturges

The Magnificent Seven is a remake of Akira Kurosawa's 1954 Japanese film Seven Samurai. The story of seven plucky men pitting their forces against a virtual army of bandits is cleverly relocated to the Wild West, and although not an immediate success, this film gradually gathered a huge fan base and as a result three sequels were made. The majestic theme music by Elmer Bernstein ranks as one of the best known Western themes of all time and complements perfectly this story of the nobility of self sacrifice.

Storyline

A Mexican village is raided by bandits led by Calvera (Eli Wallach) who steal the villagers' scant supply of food. Riding off, Calvera taunts the terrified villagers, promising he will return to rob them again. Desperate to defend themselves, the village leaders ride to a nearby American town hoping to barter goods for weapons. The veteran gunslinger, Chris (Yul Brynner), hears of the villagers' plight, and tells them to hire gunfighters as this would be cheaper that buying weapons. The villagers beg Chris to become their gunman and he agrees to help them in spite of the fact that they can pay him very little.

Chris recruits six other gunmen for this mission: the enthusiastic but inexperienced Chico (Horst Buchholz); Chris's friend Harry Luck (Brad Dexter); drifter Vin (Steve McQueen); Irish-Mexican gunfighter

Bernardo O'Reilly (Charles Bronson); the adventure-seeking cowboy Britt (James Coburn), and a fugitive gunman, Lee (Robert Vaughn). This hotchpotch groups known it cannot defeat Calvera's gang, as they are heavily outnumbered, but hopes that Calvera will move on to a softer target when he discovers that the village is willing to defend itself.

The seven men arrive at the village and begin to teach the villagers how to fight. They quickly bond with the farmers and their wives, who share their meagre supply of food with their defenders, and young Chico becomes infatuated with Petra (Rosenda

Monteros). Calvera and his bandits arrive and are run out of town by the gunmen and the villagers. Mexican Chico follows Calvera to his camp and discovers that Calvera has been compelled to raid the village because he and his men are starving. Chico reports this news to the gunmen, who ride out to confront Calvera at his camp. The camp is deserted, and upon returning to the village the gunmen discover that the terrified villagers have surrendered control of the village to Calvera. Fearing reprisals from the US army, Calvera does not kill the gunmen but instead banishes them from the village.

The gunmen debate what should be done. Harry says that further action is suicidal and rides off, but the others decide to fight to liberate the village. When the gunmen attack Calvera and his men, they are soon joined by the grateful villagers. Bernardo dies protecting the children he had befriended, and Britt and Lee perish after having killed a considerable number of bandits. As the gunfight rages, Harry makes a surprise return and is shot dead while protecting his old friend, Chris. Eventually the gunmen and the villagers overpower the bandits and Chris shoots Calvera.

Dying, Calvera asks why Chris would risk his life to help destitute peasants.

Only three of the gunmen are left alive, and solemnly they begin to bury their fallen comrades and the villagers who fought alongside them. Chris and Vin ride out, but Chico remains in the village with his beloved Petra. As they ride away, Chris observes that the only victors of this campaign were the farmers: gunmen always lose.

Bullet points

- Elmer Bernstein's score references classical music, including Bartok's Concerto for Orchestra.

- Three sequels were made: Return of the Seven (1966); Guns of the Magnificent Seven (1969), and The Magnificent Seven Ride (1972).

- In 2013 the film was selected for preservation in the United States National Film Registry by the Library of Congress as being 'culturally, historically, or aesthetically significant'.

THE MAGNIFICENT SEVEN

They fought like seven hundred

E McQUEEN   **JAMES COBURN** "BRITT"   **HORST BUCHHOLZ** "CHICO"   **YUL BRYNNER** "CHRIS ADAMS"   **BRAD DEXTER** "HARRY LUCK"   **ROBERT VAUGHN** "LEE"   **CHARLES BRONSO** "BERNARDO O'REI

The Man from Laramie (1955)

Director: Anthony Mann

66Danger was this man's specialty" - so
says the chart-topping theme song from
The Man from Laramie, performed by Jimmy
Young. Based on a story of the same title
by Thomas T. Flynn, first published in *The
Saturday Evening Post* in 1954, and then as
a novel in 1955, *The Man from Laramie* was
one of the first Westerns to capture the
drama of the landscape using CinemaScope.

Storyline

Will Lockhart (James Stewart) travels
from Laramie to the isolated
western town of Coronado to deliver
supplies. Lockart has more than this delivery
on his mind: his brother, a cavalry trooper,
has been killed during an Apache attack
at Dutch Creek, and Lockhart is trying to
discover more about a man rumoured to be
selling repeating rifles to the local Apaches.
Lockhart soon finds himself at loggerheads
with the powerful ranching family, the
Waggonmans, headed by cattle baron Alec
Waggoman (Donald Crisp). Alec is in a
sorry state: gradually losing his eyesight
and unable to rely upon his aggressive and
obstinate son, Dave (Alex Nicol), Alec
is plagued by dreams of a stranger who
intends to kill his son.

Alec's niece, Barbara Waggoman
(Cathy O'Donnell), tells Lockhart that he is
welcome to help himself to salt, but when
Dave sees Lockhart hauling the salt away
he accuses him of theft and shoots twelve of
Lockhart's mules and sets fire to his wagons.
Back in town, Lockhart ends up in a fist fight,
first with Dave and then with ranch foreman
Vic Hansbro (Arthur Kennedy). Alec arrives
and defuses the situation, offering Lockhart

compensation for his mules and wagons.

Alec holds Vic responsible for the damage that Dave caused to Lockhard's mules and wagons, and threatens to withhold the $600 compensation money from his pay, in spite of the fact that Vic is engaged to be married to Barbara and is practically a member of the family. Hurt and angry, Vic rides after Dave and catches him attempting to contact the Apaches to arrange the delivery of two hundred repeating rifles. Vic shoots Dave and frames Lockhart for his murder.

Rival rancher, Kate Canady (Aline MacMahon), offers Lockhart sanctuary, and urges him to negotiate a truce with Alec. Alec meanwhile begins to suspect that his son was, indeed, selling rifles to the Apaches: going over some old bills he comes across the receipt for a wildly overpriced fence that he thinks conceals a rifle purchase. Although Vic tries to persuade him to let it go, Alec is determined to discover the truth. In desperation Vic tries to detain Alec, and accidentally pushes him off his horse and down a hill. Thinking he has killed Alec, Vic rides off.

Alec survives the fall: having been found by Lockhart he is nursed back to health by Kate. Grateful to Lockhart, Alec reveals that it was Dave who sold the Apaches the rifles that killed Lockhart's brother.

Determined to settle matters, Lockhart rides out and discovers Vic using a smoke signal to summon the Apaches to come for their rifles. Unable to shoot a man in cold blood, Lockhart makes Vic push the wagon off a hilltop to destroy the rifles and then lets him ride away. The Apaches who paid for the rifles confront Vic and kill him when he fails to deliver the goods.

Lockhart reveals to the grieving Barbara that he is Captain Lockhart, a cavalry officer in the U.S. Army. Barbara tells Lockhart that she intends to leave Coronado and head back east, and he tells her to ask for Captain Lockhart when she passes through Laramie.

Bullet points

- Actor James Stewart, who plays Captain Lockhart in *The Man from Laramie*, was a real life military hero who received numerous medals for acts of valour.

- The film's director, Anthony Mann, was the original director of *Spartacus* (1960) but was replaced by Stanley Kubrick early in production after being fired by the film's producer and star, Kirk Douglas.

The Man Who Shot Liberty Valance (1962)

Director: John Ford

Ford chose to film The Man Who Shot Liberty Valance in black and white, rather than his usual brilliant colour, to create greater atmosphere. Widely considered to be one of Ford's best Westerns, The Man Who Shot Liberty Valance is a tender and thought provoking treatise on U.S. democracy.

Storyline

U.S. Senator Ransom "Ranse" Stoddard (James Stewart) and his wife Hallie (Vera Miles) arrive in Shinbone to attend the funeral of Tom Doniphon (John Wayne). Intrigued, the local newspaper reporter asks Stoddard why a Senator would travel so far for the funeral of a rancher.

As Stoddard begins to explain, we are taken back in time: Stoddard is an eager young attorney who has been advised to "Go West" and duly taken the stagecoach to Shinbone. Outside town the stagecoach is robbed by a gang led by the whip cracking gunfighter Liberty Valance (Lee Marvin) who violently assaults Stoddard and leaves him for dead. Unconscious, he is found by rancher Tom Doniphon (John Wayne) and his ranch hand Pompey (Woody Strode) and taken to recuperate at the restaurant run by Hallie and her parents. Marshal Link Appleyard (Andy Devine) arrives but makes it clear that he is terrified of Valance and has no intention of arresting him. Stoddard insists that the law must be upheld, but Doniphon dismisses this as fantasy: out West, a man relies upon his gun, not the law.

Left destitute by the robbery, Stoddard washes dishes to earn his keep at the restaurant. Valance turns up and humiliates the "lawyer", and Doniphon advises Stoddard to get a gun or get out of town. Stoddard declares that he will stay and open a law firm. Although he gets no clients, he opens a successful school to teach members of the community to read. Aware he is in danger, Stoddard attempts to learn how to shoot, and is humiliated when Doniphon demonstrates his vast superiority with a gun.

Local newspaper owner Dutton Peabody (Edmond O'Brien) publishes a story about the cattle barons' opposition to the territory's statehood and Stoddard explains to his pupils that statehood will ensure safety, education and investment in infrastructure. Shinbone's residents meet to elect two delegates for the statehood convention. Valance and his henchmen (Lee Van Cleef and Strother Martin) burst into the meeting and attempt to intimidate the assembly into electing Valance as a delegate, but the residents elect Stoddard and Peabody instead. Humiliated, Valance gives Stoddard two options: meet him for a

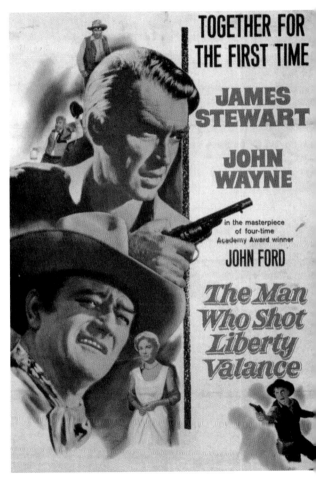

duel that night or get out of town.

Valance and his men ransack Peabody's newspaper office and beat him unconscious after he publishes news of Valance's election defeat. Stoddard had been planning to leave town, but hearing of Peabody's injuries he decides to stay to confront Valance. In the darkened street they prepare for their duel. Valance disarms Stoddard by shooting him in the arm. Valance tells Stoddard to pick up his gun with his other hand, and Stoddard shoots him dead. Doniphon, who is in love with Hallie, is heartbroken to see her lovingly bathing Stoddard's wound. Realising that she does not love him, Doniphon burns down the house he had been building as a wedding gift to Hallie.

Shinbone residents attend the territorial convention for statehood, and Stoddard feels ashamed when opponents point out that his only claim to fame is killing a man. Doniphon tells Stoddard that is was he who shot Valance: hiding in an alley, Doniphon killed Valance because he knew that Hallie loved Stoddard, and above all else he wants Hallie to be happy. Doniphon tells him to make Hallie happy by winning the election.

The flashback ends. Stoddard tells the news reporter that he married Hallie and had a glittering career in politics, in spite of not being a sharp shooter. The reporter burns his notes, saying "This is the West, sir. When the legend becomes fact, print the legend". Stoddard, rather than Doniphon, will go down in history as the man who shot Liberty Valance.

Bullet points

- Burt Bacharach and Hal David wrote a song based upon the film, called "The Man Who Shot Liberty Valance". Recorded by Gene Pitney it became a Top 10 hit but was not used in the film.

- Legendary Western director Sergio Leone named The Man Who Shot Liberty Valance as his favourite John Ford film.

- In 2007, the film was selected for preservation in the United States National Film Registry by the Library of Congress as being 'culturally, historically, or aesthetically significant'.

The Missing (2003)

Director: Ron Howard

The Missing is commonly described as a Revisionist Western, which is a subgenre of the Western that attempts to offer a grittier, more realistic depiction of life in the Wild West and often features strong female characters. *The Missing* is based on the 1996 novel by Thomas Eidson, *The Last Ride*, and is notable for its authentic use of the Apache language by various actors, some of whom spent many hours studying it. A dark tale of abduction and ritualistic murder, *The Missing* is softened by its portrayal of the power of family love.

Storyline

It is the late nineteenth century, New Mexico. Samuel Jones (Tommy

Lee Jones) turns up at the home of his daughter Maggie Gilkeson (Cate Blanchett) hoping for a reconciliation after many years' absence, but she rebuffs him. Meanwhile, Pesh–Chidin and a dozen of his followers are ritualistically killing settlers and kidnapping their daughters to sell into slavery in Mexico. The U.S. Cavalry is refusing to help parents retrieve their daughters as its troops are busy conducting a forced relocation of captured Native Americans, so when Maggie's daughter Lilly (Evan Rachel Wood) is captured by Pesh-Chidin, Maggie reluctantly accepts her father's offer to help find her.

Maggie, her father, and Maggie's younger daughter Dot (Jenna Boyd) set out to track the attackers, and come across Kayitah (Jay Tavare) and his son

Honesco (Simon R. Baker). Kayitah is an old friend of Jones, and tells the group that he too is tracking the attackers, who have abducted his son's fiancée. Maggie treats Kayitah's injuries and the families decide to join forces to hunt for the missing girls. Kayitah is a Chiricahua, and tells Maggie that her father had once been a member of their Chiricahua band, and was given the name Chaa–dud–ba–its–iidan ("Shit for Luck") during their wanderings.

United, the two families free the girls, but Kayitah is killed and the families are pursued into the mountains by the determined kidnappers. Realising that they cannot run forever, the two families engage in a fight with the kidnappers: during this battle, Jones fights the Pesh-Chidin (Eric Schweig), the man who kidnapped his granddaughter Lilly. Pesh-Chidin attempts to kill Maggie with a pistol and Jones sacrifices his life to save her by wrestling Pesh-Chidin off a cliff and falling to his death alongside him. Maggie scares off the last remaining kidnappers by shooting at them. Her family has been reunited, but she has lost her father: understanding now the depth of his love for her, Maggie finally forgives him for past wrongs.

Bullet points

☞ Director Ron Howard spent six years playing the teenage Richie Cunningham in the popular sitcom *Happy Days*, which aired from 1974–1984.

☞ Tommy Lee Jones, who plays Samuel Jones in the film, played Texas Ranger Woodrow F. Call in the award-winning Western TV miniseries, *Lonesome Dove*, originally broadcast in 1989.

The Outlaw Josey Wales (1976)

Director: Clint Eastwood

The Outlaw Josey Wales was inspired by a 1972 novel by Forrest Carter and was originally titled *The Rebel Outlaw: Josey Wales* and later re-titled *Gone to Texas*. Eastwood describes this as an anti-war film that demonstrates how combat unites people yet destroys them at the same time. *The Outlaw Josey Wales* references lines from the Bible, "Those who use the sword shall die by the sword" (Matthew 26:52). On a literal level, the man who drew his sword against Wales (played by director Clint Eastwood) is killed by that same sword, but on a deeper level this powerful film shows how revenge cannot bring loved ones back from the grave. The great Chinese philosopher Confucius said, "Before you embark on a journey of revenge, dig two graves". Again, on a literal level, Wales digs two graves, one for his wife, the other for his son, but of course, this is not what Confucius meant, and we see the wisdom of his words played out at the close of the film: in seeking revenge, Wales has metaphorically killed himself.

Storyline

The wife and son of Missouri farmer, Josey Wales (Clint Eastwood) have been murdered by a band of pro-Union Jayhawers, or guerilla fighters. Wales buries his family and marks their humble graves with a cross. In tears, Wales leans against the cross and his silhouette forms the "St Andrew's" cross of the Confederacy Battle Flag, symbolising Wales' change of allegiance from the Union to the Confederacy.

Seeking to avenge his family, Wales joins a group of pro-Confederate Missouri Bushwhackers led by William T. Anderson, also known as "Bloody Bill" (John Russell). The American Civil War ends and Captain Fletcher (John Vernon) persuades the guerrillas to surrender, saying they have been granted amnesty. This is a trick: Captain Terrill's (Bill McKinney) Redlegs massacre the surrendering men. Wales, who refused to surrender, intervenes and kills several Redlegs with a Gatling gun and has his faced slashed by Terrill's sword. Senator Lane, leader of the Kansas Brigade, puts a $5,000 bounty on Wales.

On the run from the Union militia, Wales picks up a number of companions including an old Cherokee named Lone Watie (Chief Dan George) and a group of Navajo women that Wales rescued from Comancheros. In Texas, Wales and his companions come under attack from the Redlegs but are gunned down by Wales' band: out of ammunition, Wales rides after the fleeing Captain Terrill and stabs him with the same cavalry sword that Terrill used to slash his face.

Fletcher, accompanied by two Texas Rangers, turns up at a bar in Santa Rio, where the injured Wales is drinking. The locals at the bar tell the Rangers that Wales

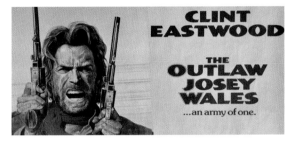

was killed in a shoot-out in Monterrey, Mexico. Believing this story, the Rangers prepare to move on, and although Fletcher has secretly recognised Wales, he declares his intention to travel to Mexico to find Wales and try to convince him that the war is over. Seeing blood dripping on Wales' boot, Fletcher says that he will give Wales the first move, because he "owes him that". Wales agrees, saying that they all died a little in the war. Wales then rides off.

Bullet points

- Eastwood's seven-year-old son Kyle Eastwood appears in the film.

- In 1996, the film was deemed 'culturally, historically, or aesthetically significant' and selected for preservation in the National Film Registry of the Library of Congress.

The Searchers (1956)

Director: John Ford

Based on the the 1954 novel by Alan Le May, the plot of *The Searchers* shares similarities with the true life story of Cynthia Ann Parker, who was kidnapped by Comanche warriors when she was just nine years old. Cynthia spent twenty-four years with the Comanches, during which time she married a war chief and had three children. Cynthia's uncle never gave up searching for her, and 1860 she was rescued against her will by Texas Rangers. While capturing the urgency of the search for a missing child, *The Searchers* also confronts the issue of racism: when John Wayne's character declares he would rather see his niece dead than living as an Indian, the absurdity of bigotry is laid bare. In 2008 *The Searchers* was named the Greatest American Western of all time by the American Film Institute.

Storyline

Three years after the end of the American Civil War, Confederate veteran Ethan Edwards (John Wayne) returns to the home of his brother Aaron (Walter Coy) in west Texas. Shortly after his arrival, Ethan and a group of Rangers led by Captain Samuel Clayton (Ward Bond) set off to investigate the theft of some cattle, only to discover that this was a ploy by the Comanches to lure the men away from home. Arriving back at the house they discover that the Comanches have murdered Aaron alongside his wife and son and kidnapped Debbie (played as a child by Lana Wood) and her older sister Lucy (Pippa Scott).

After a hurried funeral, the men set off in pursuit of the Comanches. Along the way they discover the graves of Comanches killed during the raid, and the bitter Ethan mutilates a corpse. The Rangers survive an Indian attack, but with too few men to ensure victory, Clayton and the posse return home, leaving Ethan to continue his search for the girls with Lucy's fiancé Brad Jorgensen (Harry Carey, Jr.) and Debbie's adopted brother Martin Pawley (Jeffrey Hunter). Ethan finds Lucy's body dumped in a canyon near the Comanche camp: distraught,

Brad charges into the camp and is killed.

Ethan receives a letter from a man named Futterman (Peter Mamokos) and travels with Martin to Futterman's trading post, where he informs them that Debbie has been taken by Scar (Henry Brandon), the chief of the Nawyecka band of Comanches. After looking for Debbie at a military fort, Ethan and Martin go to New Mexico, where a Mexican leads them to Scar's camp. Five years after her abduction, they finally find Debbie (Natalie Wood). Now living as one of Scar's wives, Debbie tells her uncle and adopted brother than she has become a Comanche and asks them to leave without her. Ethan declares that he would rather see her dead than living as an Indian and tries to shoot her. Martin shields Debbie and a Comanche shoots Ethan with an arrow. The men escape: furious that he tried to kill Debbie, Martin says he wishes Ethan were dead, to which Ethan replies, "That'll be the day". Their quest apparently over, the men return home.

Martin discovers that Charlie McCorry (Ken Curtis) has been courting his sweetheart Laurie (Vera Miles) in his absence: arriving home as their wedding is about to commence, Martin and Charlie engage in a fistfight. Lt. Greenhill (Patrick Wayne) arrives with information about the whereabouts of Scar. Clayton leads his men to the Comanche camp where they plan to launch a direct attack. Martin sneaks into the camp and rescues Debbie and kills Scar, who is then scalped by Ethan. Instead of killing Debbie, Ethan carries her home. Martin is reunited with his sweetheart Laurie, and Ethan heads back to his house. The cabin door closes upon his receding image.

Bullet points

- British band "The Searchers" named themselves after the film.

- In *Saving Private Ryan* (1998), Steven Spielberg pays homage to the famous doorway shot when the Army brings the news of the death of Private Ryan's three brothers to their mother.

- In 1989, *The Searchers* was deemed 'culturally, historically, or aesthetically significant' by the United States Library of Congress, and was selected for preservation in its National Film Registry.

The Wild Bunch (1969)

Director: Sam Peckinpah

Peckinpah uses the Wild West as a vehicle to raise questions about how violence begets violence in his masterpiece, *The Wild Bunch,* which was filmed during the contentious and bloody Vietnam War. Peckinpah wanted to give his audience some idea of what it is like to be gunned down, and the film's hyper-violence was partly inspired by director Arthur Penn's box-office hit, *Bonnie and Clyde* (1967). A stickler for detail, Peckinpah insisted on each type of firearm used in the film having a unique sound effect when fired, and this bloodbath of a film has been described as poetic and a symphony of death. Not for the fainthearted, *The Wild Bunch* is one of the grittiest Westerns of all time.

Storyline

It is Texas in 1913, and Pike Bishop (William Holden) is the leader of a gang of aging outlaws. Pike plans to retire after one last job stealing silver from a railroad office. This job goes badly wrong: the gang is ambushed by Pike's former partner, Deke Thornton (Robert Ryan) and a posse of bounty hunters hired by the railroad. A street parade shields Pike, but many citizens are killed in the crossfire. Pike rides off with only surviving members of his gang: Dutch Engstrom (Ernest Borgnine), brothers Lyle (Warren Oates) and Tector Gorch (Ben Johnson), and Angel (Jaime Sánchez). They open the cache of silver, only to discover that it has been substituted by steel washers. Bitterly disappointed, the gang reunite with old-

timer Freddie Sykes (Edmond O'Brien) and head for Mexico.

After crossing the Rio Grande the men spent the night in Angel's birthplace, which is now ruled by the homicidal Mexican general Mapache (Emilio Fernández). Pike's gang makes contact with the general, but when Angel spots a former lover in an embrace with Mapache he loses his cool and shoots her dead, angering Mapache. Defusing the situation, Pike offers to work for Mapache, and is commissioned to steal weapons from a U.S. Army train. The men are offered a cache of gold coins for this job, and Angel says he will give his share to Pike if he agrees to send one crate of the stolen weapons to rebels opposed to Mapache. The train robbery goes according to plan, but Deke and his posse reappear and chase the gang to the border.

Aware that they risk being double-crossed by Mapache, Pike and his men devise a safe means of delivering the stolen weapons, but the mother of the woman killed by Angel tells Mapache that he has pilfered some of the weapons, and Angel is duly captured and tortured by Mapache's troops. Pike's gang returns to "Agua Verde" where a feast to celebrate the weapons transfer is under way, and they see the barely-conscious Angel being dragged by a rope tied behind the General's car. Pike and his gang try to persuade Mapache to release Angel, and he pretends to consent to their request, but sadistically slits Angel's throat instead. Enraged, Pike and his men gun Mapache down in front of his soldiers, who are too surprised to take immediate action. Pike turns his gun on the German officer who is acting as a military advisor to Mapache and kills him too. Mayhem erupts: with machine guns blazing Pike and his men are slain alongside many Mexicans.

Deke finally catches up with Pike's gang, and permits his posse to gather up their corpses in order to collect the reward money from the railroad. The posse rides off, but knowing what is likely to happen to them, Deke stays behind. After a while, Sykes arrives with the band of Mexican rebels armed by Angel. Sure enough, they have butchered Deke's posse on the way. Sykes invites Deke to come along with them and join the Mexican Revolution. Smiling, Deke agrees.

Bullet points

- *The Wild Bunch* is noted for its use of normal and slow motion images, a revolutionary cinema technique in 1969.

- Actor Lee Marvin was offered a role in the film but pulled out after he was offered more money to star in *Paint Your Wagon* (1969).

- In 1999, the U.S. National Film Registry selected The Wild Bunch for preservation in the Library of Congress for being 'culturally, historically, and aesthetically significant'.

3:10 to Yuma (1957)

Director: Delmer Daves

3:10 to Yuma is a Western thriller based on a 1953 short story by Elmore Leonard. An instant hit with audiences, this tense and exhilarating film inspired an equally successful remake in 2007 starring Russell Crow and Christian Bale.

Storyline

Arizona Territory; the 1880s. Ben Wade (Glenn Ford) and his gang rob a stagecoach and kill the driver; a crime witnessed by rancher Dan Evans (Van Heflin). Posing as cowhands, Wade and his gang stop at a saloon in Bisbee. Wade is captured but his gang is still at large: fearing that Wade's gang will attempt to rescue him, the town marshal decides to have two volunteers escort him to Contention City to board the 3:10 train to Yuma. This is a dangerous job, so the stage-line owner, Mr Butterfield (Robert Emhardt), declares that the escorts will receive $200. Poor and desperate, Dan is eager to take the job, but the only other volunteer is the town drunk, Alex Potter (Henry Jones). Reluctantly, the marshal hires them.

Wade is taken to Dan's ranch and invited to supper by his wife Alice (Leora Dana). During the night, Dan and Alex escort Wade to Contention City and head to the hotel's bridal suite hired by Butterfield. Bob Moons (Sheridan Comerate), the brother of the stagecoach driver killed by Wade, suddenly appears and threatens to avenge his brother's murder. Dan wrestles Moons' gun away from him but it goes off during the struggle. Downstairs, gang member

Charlie Prince (Richard Jaeckel) hears the gunshot: spotting Wade in a window he rides off to fetch the rest of the gang. Butterfield has hired five additional men to help Dan and Alex get Wade onboard the train, but when they see seven riders enter town they quit, leaving the trio to manage Dan alone.

Alex goes outside to see what is happening and the spots one of Wade's gang on the roof opposite the hotel: Alex yells a warning to Dan and is shot in the back by a gang member. The callous gang kill Alex by hanging him from the hotel chandelier Butterfield reckons that Wade is not worth dying for and tells Dan that he is free to quit this job. Fearing that her husband Dan is in danger, Alice arrives in town and begs him to come home, but Dan is determined to honour Alex's sacrifice by completing their mission.

The clock strikes three: Dan escorts Wade out of the backdoor under a volley of gunfire. Dodging the bullets they reach the station where the train is waiting. Wade's gang confronts Dan on the platform as the train starts to leave. Charlie tells Wade to duck so that they can get a clear shot of Dan, but instead Wade surprises everyone by telling Dan to jump with him into the passing baggage car. As the train pulls out of the station it is pursued by Wade's gang: Dan shoots Charlie and the others give up the chase.

Wade explains that he saved Dan's life because he owed him a favour after Dan protected him from Bob Moons. Besides, Wade has broken out of Yuma jail before, and is confident he will do so again. Alice sees that Dan is safe on the train, and is relieved.

Bullet points

☞ The title song "3:10 to Yuma" was written by George Duning (music) and Ned Washington (lyrics) and was performed by Frankie Laine.

☞ In 2012, the film was selected for preservation in the United States National Film Registry by the Library of Congress as being 'culturally, historically, or aesthetically significant'.

Tombstone (1993)

Director: George P. Cosmatos

Tombstone is a fictional account of the exploits of the real life Western lawman, Wyatt Earp, who has passed into legend for his part in the showdown with the Clantons at the O.K. Corral. As in other films about Wyatt Earp, such as *My Darling Clementine* (1946), the relationship between Wyatt and his consumptive friend, the gambler and gunslinger Doc Holliday, is central to the narrative. Actor Val Kilmer has been praised for his portrayal of Holliday as a man who is witty and reflective but above all else brave: *Tombstone* is an epic portrayal of the value of friendship and courage under fire.

Storyline

It is Arizona, the 1880s. Retired lawman Wyatt Earp (Kurt Russell) and his brothers Virgil (Sam Elliott) and Morgan (Bill Paxton) decide to settle down in the small mining town of Tombstone, where Wyatt is reunited with his old friend Doc Holliday (Val Kilmer), a gambler and gunslinger stricken with tuberculosis and alcoholism. When a travelling theatre arrives in town, Wyatt finds himself attracted to the lovely Josephine Marcus (Dana Delany) while his wife Mattie (Dana Wheeler-Nicholson) grows ever more dependent on laudanum.

"Curly Bill" Brocius (Powers Boothe) is the leader of a gang of outlaws known as the Cowboys who identify themselves by wearing red sashes. Wyatt tells Curly that he is no longer interested in enforcing the law, but takes him into custody when Curly kills the marshal. Curly stands trial and is released due to lack of witnesses. Enraged, Virgil becomes the new marshal and imposes a weapons ban within the Tombstone city limits. A gunfight ensues at the O.K. Corral: some Cowboys are killed and Virgil and Morgan are injured. County sheriff Johnny Behan (Jon Tenney) is in league with the Cowboys, and in retribution for the Cowboys' massacre the Wyatt brothers are ambushed.

With Morgan dead and Virgil injured, Wyatt proclaims that he is a U.S. Marshal and swears to kill any man he sees wearing a red sash. Wyatt and Doc join forces with a small band of men to enforce the law, but this posse is ambushed by the Cowboys: Wyatt shoots Curly dead, whereupon Johnny Ringo (Michael Biehn) becomes the leader of the Cowboys.

Doc's health is deteriorating, so Wyatt takes him to Henry Hooker's (Charlton Heston) ranch where Wyatt is delighted to encounter the lovely Josephine. Ringo sends a messenger to the ranch towing the corpse of one Wyatt's posse members, and he tells them that Ringo wants a showdown with Wyatt, who agrees. Doc is a far superior gunfighter and wants to take Wyatt's place, but Wyatt says he is too sick.

Not realising that Doc has already concealed himself at the location of the showdown, Wyatt arrives to confront Ringo. Doc shoots and kills Ringo, and

A George P. Cosmatos Film

TOMBSTONE

together with Wyatt hunts and kills the remaining Cowboys. Deathly sick, Doc enters a sanatorium in Glenwood Springs, Colorado. Wyatt visits his old friend, who urges him to go after Josephine. The narrator informs us that Wyatt and Josephine had a long and happy marriage that ended with Wyatt's death in Los Angeles in 1929.

Bullet points

- The film's score, composed and produced by Bruce Broughton, references the soundtrack of the classic Western *The Searchers* (1956).

- Actor Robert Mitchum was originally cast as Newman Haynes Clanton, but when he suffered a horse riding accident which left him unable to work this part was written out and he narrated the film instead.

True Grit (1969)

Director: Henry Hathaway

Based on Charles Portis' 1968 novel, *True Grit,* veteran Western actor John Wayne won his only Academy Award for his stellar performance as U.S. Marshal Reuben J. "Rooster" Cogburn. The friendship that develops between the one-eyed doughty marshal and the feisty young girl who demands retribution for her father's death is both amusing and highly affective. In 2010, Joel and Ethan Coen released their own stunning version of *True Grit* starring Jeff Bridges, Matt Damon and Hailee Steinfeld.

Storyline

It is 1878, Arkansas, and Frank Ross (John Pickard) has been murdered by his hired hand, Tom Chaney (Jeff Corey). Ross' 14-year-old daughter Mattie (Kim Darby) travels to Fort Smith to hire a marshal to capture Chaney. Mattie chooses the aging U.S. Marshal Reuben "Rooster" J. Cogburn (John Wayne) after hearing that Cogburn has "true grit". She gives Rooster a down payment to track down Chaney, who has escaped into Indian Territory with "Lucky" Ned Pepper (Robert Duvall) and his gang.

Mattie and Rooster are joined by a young Texas Ranger, La Boeuf (Glen Campbell), who hopes to collect a $1,500 reward for apprehending Chaney for the murder of a Texas senator. La Boeuf is a braggart, but the reward money he is after is far greater than the $75 reward offered by Mattie, so Rooster decides to pair up with him. The men try to abandon Mattie, but she is determined to stick with them.

After several days, they arrive at a cabin occupied by two horse thieves, Emmett Quincy (Jeremy Slate) and Moon (Dennis Hopper). Moon's leg is badly injured and Rooster uses the injury to extract information about Pepper. Quincy silences Moon by stabbing him, whereupon Rooster kills Quincy.

Before Moon dies, he tells Rooster that Pepper and his gang are due at the hideout that night.

After laying in wait, Rooster and La Boeuf attack and kill two gang members but Pepper and the others escape. Rooster, La Boeuf and Mattie go to McAlester's store. Fearing for her safety, Rooster tries to persuade Mattie to stay at McAlester's, but she refuses. A few days later, Mattie loses her footing on the way down a steep hill and comes face-to-face with Chaney. Calling out to Rooster and La Boeuf, Mattie shoots and wounds Chaney but is captured by Pepper and his gang.

Rooster attacks Pepper and his gang while La Boeuf captures Chaney and rescues Mattie. Rooster tells Pepper he has a choice: get killed now or surrender and be hanged. Pepper scoffs that this is "bold talk for a one-eyed fat man" who is outnumbered 4:1. Enraged, Rooster puts his horse's rein in his mouth, takes a Colt.45 in one hand and his Winchester in the other and charges at the four gang members, shooting dead three and wounding Pepper. Pepper shoots Rooster's horse, which falls and traps him. Helpless, Rooster is about to be shot by Pepper when he is saved by La Boeuf, who kills Pepper at a distance of 400 yards with a magnificent shot from his Sharps carbine.

Suddenly, Chaney leaps out from behind a tree and crashes a rock onto La Boeuf's head. Mattie shoots and wounds Chaney, but is knocked backwards by the recoil and falls into a pit where she is bitten by a rattlesnake. Rooster kills Chaney and descends into the pit to rescue Mattie. La Boeuf regains consciousness and ties a rope to his horse to pull Rooster and Mattie out of the pit, then collapses and dies. Desperate to get help for Mattie, Rooster rides so frantically that the horse drops dead beneath him, whereupon Rooster scoops up Mattie and runs with her in his arms until he encounters horsemen with a wagon. With no time to explain, Rooster steals the wagon and rides it to McAlester's, where an Indian doctor treats Mattie's snakebite and sets her broken arm. A few days later, Mattie's attorney arrives and directed by Mattie he gives Rooster the reward money plus $200 for saving Mattie's life.

Sometime later Rooster visits Mattie at her home. Mattie asks Rooster to promise that when he dies he will be buried beside her family. Reluctantly, he agrees. As he leaves, Rooster leaps over a fence with his new horse to show Mattie he is not so old after all.

Bullet points

- The horse shown during the final scene of *True Grit* was Dollor, John Wayne's favorite horse.

- In 1975, John Wayne starred in the sequel, *Rooster Cogburn*.

Ulzana's Raid (1972)

Director: Robert Aldrich

Ulzana's Raid depicts a wild and bloody chase across Arizona by U.S. army troops in pursuit of indigenous Apache warriors, and this dark film has been described as an allegory of the United States' participation in the highly contentious Vietnam War. Hailed by many as the greatest Western of the 1970s, *Ulzana's Raid* is unflinching in its portrayal of the agony of conscience that may beset a solider even when he is confronting the most brutal of enemies.

Storyline

It is the 1880s, Arizona. Resentful of their mistreatment by agency authorities, Ulzana (Joaquín Martínez) and a small war party of Chiricahua Apaches break out of the San Carlos Indian Reservation. The military commander dispatches messengers to warn the local white settlers, but they are ambushed by the war party. Rather than face capture, one of the messengers kills the woman he is escorting and then commits suicide. Laughing, the warriors play catch with the messenger's heart. The authorities are desperate to capture Ulzana and his warriors, so ask army scout McIntosh (Burt Lancaster) to assist a troop of soldiers led by an inexperienced Lieutenant Garnett DeBuin (Bruce Davison). They are joined by a veteran sergeant (Richard Jaeckel) and an Apache army scout Ke-Ni-Tay (Jorge Luke), who is related through marriage to Ulzana

The cavalry troop leaves Fort Lowell and follows the horrific trail of destruction left by the Apache war party. Struggling to engage with an enemy that has vastly superior territorial knowledge, DeBuin experiences an existential crisis while McIntosh and Ke-Ni-Tay attempt to outthink and outfight the Apaches. McIntosh hatches a plan that leads to the death of Ulzana's son and the loss of the war party's horses.

The Apache war party attacks a farm and steals two horses: although they torture the settlers, they leave the farmer's wife alive so that she will be escorted to the fort by soldiers. McIntosh realises that the Apaches need more horses, and that this is a cunning ruse to ambush the mounted troops. McIntosh suggests they employ a decoy to trick Ulzana, but this plan goes awry: Ulzana and his warriors ambush the military escort and seize all the horses, but the Apaches kill most of the soldiers before DeBuin can arrive with his forces, and McIntosh is mortally wounded. Ke-Ni-Tay scatters the captured horses, and Ulzana escapes on foot while his war party is routed by DeBuin's men. Ke-Ni-Tay catches up with Ulzana, and shows him the bugle taken from his dead son. Ulzana lays down his weapons and sings his death song before Ke-Ni-Tay kills him. The soldiers want to take Ulzana's

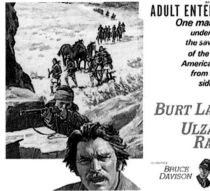

head to the fort as a trophy, but DeBuin orders him to be buried. Realising that he will not survive the journey back to the fort, McIntosh decides to stay behind.

Bullet points

- Director Robert Aldrich is best known for his sci-fi and horror films, such as *Kiss Me Deadly* (1955) and *What Ever Happened to Baby Jane* (1962).

- In 1999, Burt Lancaster, who plays McIntosh in the film, was named 19th greatest male star of all time by the American Film Institute.

Unforgiven (1992)

Director: Clint Eastwood

"To err is human; to forgive, divine." Alexander Pope's famous maxim is tested to its limits in *Unforgiven*, which stars Clint Eastwood as a man who has forsaken alcohol and violence only to return to his old ways in order to forge a better future for his children. *Unforgiven* is often identified as the best Western of all time, and it is easy to see why: with tense gunfights, deep friendship and humour, this film captures all that is best about the genre.

Storyline:

Big Whiskey, Wyoming. Sheriff and former gunfighter "Little" Bill Daggett (Gene Hackman) has banned firearms from town. When Little Bill fails to take action, the local prostitutes decide to offer a $1,000 reward for the assassination of Quick Mike (David Mucci) and "Davey-Boy" Bunting (Rob Campbell), a pair of lowlife cowboys who have wantonly disfigured prostitute Delilah Fitzgerald (Anna Levine).

Hearing of the reward, the cocky Schofield Kid (Jaimz Woolvett) turns up at the farm of William "Will" Munny (Clint Eastwood). Munny, like the sheriff, has a violent past that he has renounced: a former bandit and murderer, he is now a teetotal widower seeking to raise his children in peace. Munny's farm is failing, so after initially rejecting the Kid's offer, he leaves his children in charge and sets off to find the Kid, stopping en route to recruit his erstwhile partner in crime, Ned Logan

(Morgan Freeman).

Munny, Logan and the Kid arrive in Big Whiskey during a ferocious rainstorm and enter the saloon to discover the cowboys' whereabouts. Munny sits alone with a fever and is caught at this low ebb by Little Bill and his deputies, who discover that Munny is carrying a gun and viciously assault him in spite of his advanced years and sickness. Meanwhile Logan and the Kid are cavorting with the prostitutes upstairs, and escape via a window when they hear the commotion in the saloon.

This has been a sorry start: holed up in a barn outside town, the men must nurse Munny back to health.

Sometime later the trio ambush a group of cowboys and kill Bunting, but this escapade makes Logan realise that he has lost his appetite for murder, and so he decides to head home. Munny and the Kid make their way to the cowboys' ranch, where the Kid discovers Quick Mike in an outhouse and kills him. Shaken by this event, the Kid confesses to Munny that he has not killed anyone before and renounces life as a gunfighter.

The Kid's unhappiness is compounded by Little's (Tara Frederick) revelation that Logan has been ambushed and tortured to death by Little Bill's men. The true cost of revenge is, it seems, beyond measure. The Kid heads back to Kansas to deliver the reward money to Logan and Munny's families. Munny abandons his abstinence and drinks whisky from Ned's bottle, signalling his complete return to his former self, then heads into town to take revenge on Bill.

That night Logan's corpse is displayed as bait outside the saloon where Little Bill and the posse lie in wait. These theories do not intimidate Munny, who walks straight into the bar and kills

its owner. After some tense dialogue a gunfight ensues and Munny is victorious. Munny calmly tells the townsfolk that he will return and kill them if Logan is not buried with due respect and if any further prostitutes are harmed.

The film ends with Munny standing by his wife's grave at sunset. An epilogue tells us that his wife's mother is never able to fathom why her daughter married a known thief and murderer, and in so doing the film leaves unsolved the mystery of the human heart.

Bullet points:

- Eastwood dedicated the movie to deceased directors and mentors Don Siegel and Sergio Leone.

- *Unforgiven* won four Academy Awards: Best Picture; Best Director; Best Supporting Actor (Gene Hackman); Best Film Editing (Joel Cox).

- In 2004, *Unforgiven* was deemed 'culturally, historically, or aesthetically significant' and added to the United States National Film Registry.

CLINT EASTWOOD   GENE HACKMAN   MORGAN FREEMAN   RICHARD HARRIS

UNFORGIVEN

Vera Cruz (1954)

Director: Robert Aldrich

Vera Cruz was condemned by 1950s' film critics for its display of gratuitous violence and savagery, such as the scene where Burt Lancaster's character threatens to murder some children. Aldrich's unflinching depiction of brutality influenced future Westerns such as Sam Peckinpah's blood-soaked masterpiece, *The Wild Bunch* (1969). Aldrich went on to direct the equally violent Western, *Ulzana's Raid* (1972).

Storyline

It is 1866 and the Franco-Mexican War is raging. Ex-Confederate soldier Ben Trane (Gary Cooper) travels to Mexico seeking work as a mercenary, where he joins forces with Joe Erin (Burt Lancaster), an amoral gunslinger who heads a gang of merciless killers (including Ernest Borgnine, Jack Elam, Charles Bronson, and Archie Savage).

Erin and his men are recruited by Marquis Henri de Labordere (Cesar Romero) to serve the Emperor Maximilian I of Mexico (George Macready). Impressed by their astonishing display of marksmanship, the Emperor offers the men $25,000 to escort the Countess Duvarre (Denise Darcel) to the seaport city of Vera Cruz on the Gulf of Mexico. The charming Trane compliments the countess, whereupon the Emperor doubles their fee, and Erin is impressed by Trane's impudence.

While they are crossing a river, Trane and Erin notice that the stagecoach in which the countess is travelling is unusually heavy, and Erin discovers that

GARY COOPER · BURT LANCASTER
HAROLD HECHT'S presentation "VERA CRUZ" Ⓐ SUPERSCOPE

the stagecoach is loaded with six cases of gold coins. The countess informs Trane and Erin that the gold is worth $3 million and is intended pay for Maximilian's French army. The countess and the gang decide to steal the money and split it between them.

General Ramírez (Morris Ankrum) and his fellow Juarista leaders also suspect that the armed convoy is carrying more than just the countess, and make numerous attempts to ambush it. The Juarista secret agent Nina (Sarita Montiel) conspires with other groups to steal the gold, but the alliances amongst thieves dissolve as rapidly as they are made. The gold eventually reaches Vera Cruz where the Juarista fighters engage with French troops in a bloody battle for its ownership.

Erin persuades the countess to reveal the location of the ship that she has hired to transport the gold so he can steal it, but Trane arrives in time to stop him. Trane and Erin face off in a showdown and Erin dies. Leaving the gold, Trane winds his way through the dead bodies of the French and Juarista fighters, while the stricken wives and mothers of the Juarista troops search for their loved ones.

Bullet points

- Denise Darcel took to the sky in an L-5 Stinson light observation aircraft on VJ Day to witness the celebrations in her native Paris.

- Burt Lancaster, who plays the evil Joe Erin in *Vera Cruz*, went on to play the hero in *Ulzana's Raid* (1972), also directed by Robert Aldrich.

Winchester '73 (1950)

Director: Anthony Mann

In *Winchester '73,* a weapon becomes a character in its own right. Released in the same year as the other great gun-centric Western, *Colt.45* (1950), Mann's rifle film is far more serious in tone than its handgun rival and it literally outshoots the competition. Shot in black and white, *Winchester '73* is a dark study of the power of obsession: the gunman's fanatical desire for revenge and the gunman's desire to own the finest weapon of his trade make for an explosive combination in this epic film.

Storyline

It is 1876, and Lin McAdam (James Stewart) and friend "High-Spade" Frankie Wilson (Millard Mitchell) pursue outlaw "Dutch Henry" Brown (Stephen McNally) into Dodge City, Kansas. Sheriff Wyatt Earp (Will Geer) instructs Lin and High Spade to surrender their weapons to Earp's brother, Virgil, as firearms are not allowed in Dodge City. Lin spots Dutch Henry in the saloon, but the men cannot fight each other under Wyatt's watchful eye. Instead, they confront one another in a less deadly manner by taking part in the 4th July shooting competition. Lin and Dutch make it to the final two, both hoping to win the famous "Gun that Won the West", the One-of-One Thousand Winchester '73 rifle. Lin is victorious, but later that night Dutch steals the rifle and is chased out of town by Lin and High Spade.

Dutch Henry and his men ride to Riker's Bar, but realise that they have left their guns with Virgil: their only weapon is the Winchester '73. The men attempt to

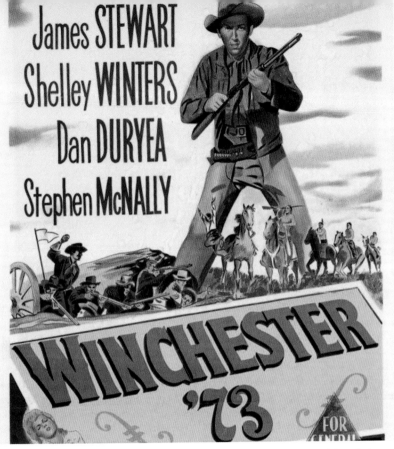

James STEWART
Shelley WINTERS
Dan DURYEA
Stephen McNALLY

WINCHESTER '73

buy guns from Indian trader Joe Lamont (John McIntire), but when he sees the magnificent Winchester '73 he raises his prices sky high. Unable to afford Joe's guns, Dutch reluctantly agrees to trade his prized rifle for $300 in gold and his choice of weapons from Joe's cache. Desperate to win back his Winchester '73, Dutch plays cards with Joe, whereupon he loses everything. Joe sells his guns to the Indians: when their leader Young Bull (Rock Hudson) catches sight of the wonderful Winchester '73 he is consumed by desire, and robs and scalps Joe when he refuses to sell it.

Meanwhile, Lola Manners (Shelley Winters) and her fiancé Steve Miller (Charles Drake) are travelling to their new home when their wagon comes under attack by Indians. Lola and Steve are saved by the Army. That night, Lin and High-Spade meet up with the soldiers and discover that their leader, Sergeant Wilkes (Jay C. Flippen) is inexperienced in fighting Indians. Lin offers Wilkes some tactical advice and gives Lola his six-gun: she understands Lin's unspoken message that she must commit suicide rather than let herself be captured by the Indians.

After a battle with the Indians, Lin and High Spade ride off in pursuit of Dutch Henry and fail to notice the Winchester '73 lying on the ground beside an Indian's corpse. Doan (Tony Curtis) picks it up and gives it to Steve: Steve and Lola ride to the Jameson house, where "Waco" Johnnie Dean (Dan Duryea) is enthralled by the magnificent rifle. Waco, who is on the run from a posse, taunts the inexperienced Steve into a gunfight and kills him. Waco seizes the Winchester '73 and escapes from the posse with Lola, seeking sanctuary

in the hideout of Dutch Henry, who promptly takes back "his" rifle.

Dutch Henry plans to commit an armed robbery in Tascosa, Texas. Lola sees Lin, and tells him that Waco is stationed in a saloon to provide cover for the gang after the robbery. Lin forces Waco to tell him where Dutch is and shoots Waco dead when he pulls his weapon on him. After chasing Dutch out of town, Lin finally confronts him on a rocky hill where a long range shootout occurs. Lin kills Dutch. High Spade tells Lola that Dutch Henry is Lin's brother-in-law: a bank robber, Dutch shot Lin's father in the back when he refused to hide his fugitive son-in-law. Lin rides back into town with his Winchester '73 to embark upon his new life with Lola.

Bullet points

- The "dead man's hand" referred to by Dutch Henry is named after the hand held by Wild Bill Hickok when he was murdered.

- Universal Pictures sponsored a contest to find the rare remaining "One-of-One Thousand" Model 1873 Winchester rifles.

**The pictures in this book were provided
courtesy of the following:**

Design & Artwork by Scott Giarnese

Published by Demand Media Limited

Publishers: Jason Fenwick & Jules Gammond

Written by Sophie Samuel

Dedicated to my son Samuel, who was born in Texas not far from the Alamo